BASIC Applications

A First Course in Structured Programming

Neville J Ford

MANCHESTER • OXFORD

British Library Cataloguing in Publication Data

Ford, Neville J.
BASIC applications: A first course in structured programming
1. Microcomputer systems. Programming languages
I. Title
005.2'6
ISBN 0-85012-771-8

© NCC BLACKWELL LTD, 1990

All rights reserved. No part of this publication may be reproduced, stored in a retrieval system, or transmitted, in any form or by any means, without the prior permission of The National Computing Centre.

Published for NCC Publications by NCC Blackwell Ltd.

Editorial Office: The National Computing Centre Limited, Oxford Road, Manchester M1 7ED, England.

NCC Blackwell Ltd, 108 Cowley Road, Oxford OX4 1JF, England.

Typeset in 10pt Times Roman by Laser 27 Limited, Manchester; and printed by Hobbs the Printers of Southampton.

ISBN 0-85012-771-8

Acknowledgements

RM BASIC is supplied by Research Machines Ltd, Oxford for use on their Nimbus computers.

IBM BASICA is supplied by International Business Machines and also known as 'Advanced BASIC'.

GW BASIC is a registered trademark of Microsoft Corp.

Turbo Basic is a trademark of Borland International Inc.

Preface

This book is derived from a lecture course to first year undergraduate students at Chester College of Higher Education. It assumes no previous knowledge of computers or programming, but it does assume that the reader has regular access to computer facilities on which to try out the exercises.

The examples in the book are based upon two versions of Basic which are currently widely available: Research Machines' RM BASIC and IBM BASICA (and similar versions, including Microsoft GW BASIC and Borland's Turbo Basic). In many example programs, more than one listing is given in order to illustrate the variations between the language implementations. As a general rule, structured (and therefore well-written) programs are more easily developed in RM and Turbo Basics than in the earlier versions.

I am grateful for the assistance given to me by two of my students: Sarah Griffiths and Elizabeth Prince, who agreed to check the manuscript for errors.

Neville Ford

Contents

	Page
Preface	
1 What is a Computer Program?	1
Introduction	1
Computer Languages	1
Background to the BASIC Language	2
Computer Programs	6
Computer Concepts	8
Acclimatisation	9
Translation	9
The Editor	11
Saving of Files	14
Don't Panic!	14
2 A First Program	15
Introduction	15
Background	15
Upper or Lower Case?	17
Bugs	17
Tidying Things Up	17
Developing the Theme	18
Exercise A	23
Elementary Calculations	24
Exercise B	25
Exercise C	25
Summary	25
3 Improve Your Presentation	27
Introduction	27

Graphics Screen Layout	27
Drawing some Simple Shapes	30
Exercise A	32
Moving PRINT and INPUT Around the Screen	32
Exercise B	35
Exercise C	39
Input and Output	39
Exercise D	42
Exercise E	42
A Real Application	43
Exercise F	45
Exercise G	53
Summary	53

4 Do it Once, and Do it Again! 55

Introduction	55
Computer Security	55
While Loops	57
Problems with the PASSWORD Program	59
Case Sensitivity	59
Exercise A	60
Controlling the Number of Failures	60
Exercise B	61
Exercise C	62
Hiding the Password	62
Exercise D	62
Summary	63

5 Come to a Party! 65

Introduction	65
Designing the Invitations	65
Exercise A	66
Making a Start on the Main Program	67
Procedure Partyinfo	68
Procedure Guestinfo — a Simplified Version	70
Procedure Invite — a Simplified Version	70
Exercise B	71
Changing the Invitation	71
The Need for Lists	71
Arrays	72
Two Types of Loop	75
Incorporating the Array into the Program	75
Exercise C	76

Exercise D	77
A Final Word About Data Security	79
Exercise E	82
Summary	82

6 Lots and Lots of Boxes — 83

Introduction	83
Why Draw Diagrams?	83
An Example Structure Diagram	85
Exercise	88
Sequence, Selection and Iteration	88
Program Design	90
Examples	90
Exercise A	96
Summary	96

7 Hello, Can I Help You? — 97

Introduction	97
Background	97
Outline Design of the System	98
The Main Driving Program	100
Catalogue Data Storage	100
Exercise A	101
The Initialisation Routine	103
Exercise B	104
Processing a Customer	105
Exercise C	108
Exercise D	110
Management Reports	111
Exercise E	122
Summary	123

8 Can I Help You Again? — 125

Introduction	125
Some Customers Wish to Buy Several Items	125
Exercise A	133
Exercise B	135
Keeping Track of Stock Levels	135
Exercise C	141
Exercise D	141
Daily Performance Records	141
Exercise E	145

Exercise F	145
Exercise G	146
Summary	146

9 A Mathematical Diversion — 147

Introduction	147
Simulations	147
Pseudo-random Numbers	148
Exercise A	150
Producing a Block Graph	150
RM BASIC	155
IBM BASICs	155
Exercise B	158
Exercise C	158
Drawing a Curve	158
Exercise D	161
Exercise E	161
Exercise F	161
Predefined Functions	162
Exercise G	162
Summary	162

10 More Advanced Topics — 163

Introduction	163
Two-dimensional Arrays	163
Exercise A	165
Random Access and Indexed Files	166
Local and Global Variables and Parameters	167
Summary	169

11 More Applications — 171

Introduction	171
How to Work on the Exercises	171
Exercise A	172
Exercise B	172
Exercise C	176
Exercise D	176
Exercise E	177
Exercise F	177
Exercise G	177

Appendix

1 Epilogue	179
2 Bibliography	181
3 Answers to Selected Exercises	183

Index 197

1 What is a Computer Program?

INTRODUCTION

In this first chapter we shall meet the concept of a computer program as a series of instructions written in a computer language. The language BASIC (Beginners All-purpose Symbolic Instruction Code) is a natural choice as a first computer language for many programmers, but other languages are available. We will distinguish between high- and low-level languages and describe the fundamental processes involved in dealing with the computers themselves, in readiness to begin programming in Chapter 2.

Computer Languages

Everyone is familiar with the idea of people from different parts of the world speaking in different languages. In order for someone to communicate effectively with another person they must use a language which they both understand. We shall see that computers too have languages which allow communication of ideas from the computer user to the machine. For this communication to be effective, both the computer and the user need to understand a common language.

Why do people speak different languages? Sometimes for historical reasons, people in different parts of the world have adopted different languages. Often as a result of experiences gained and social pressures, a variety of languages are adopted that evolve in different ways. A good example of the way in which environment affects the development of language can be seen in the existence of several Eskimo words for snow (each describing a different type of snow) while English has only the single word 'snow'.

When learning computer programming, it is normal to begin by studying 'high-level' programming languages. These are languages which have been carefully designed to be relatively easy for human programmers to understand.

As a result, they are not highly suited to the computer's hardware and so it is necessary for them to be translated either by means of an 'interpreter' or a 'compiler', before the actual instructions may be executed. We shall discuss this translation process in a little more detail later.

For many programmers today, it has become unnecessary ever to progress on to 'low-level' languages, which are close to the computer's own language, because of improvements in the available 'high-level' languages. These 'high-level' computer languages have evolved during the period since the late 1950s in reaction to changing demands from users and the changes in available hardware. Some languages which were in common use in the 1960s have now all but disappeared, with many new languages appearing; other languages have remained in use during the intervening years but have been adapted to suit newer requirements. A very few highly specialised languages have survived for many years with very few changes because they are well suited to the particular needs of their users. This hierarchy of computer languages is illustrated in Figure 1.1.

The language which forms the subject matter of this book is BASIC. BASIC is a popular language among programmers, particularly beginners, for a number of reasons:

Availability. BASIC is obtainable for almost every computer system which is currently available. In the case of some of the smaller microcomputers, BASIC is often the only high-level language which is realistically available. BASIC became widely obtainable when the microcomputer revolution allowed low cost and performance computers to appear in the shops. Both the title 'BASIC' and the usual type of 'Operating Environment' offered with BASIC systems appealed to many manufacturers of these small systems.

Cost. BASIC is frequently provided 'free' with computer systems, or is available at low cost.

Facilities. BASIC has evolved over the years to provide a wide range of facilities to suit the needs of programmers. While BASIC is often not the most suitable language in which to program a particular application, it is usually not an unreasonable choice.

Ease of use. One of the themes of this book will be the importance of the programmer making quick progress towards worthwhile goals. Among alternative languages in common use today, there are few available which provide shorter routes to early but stimulating achievements.

BACKGROUND TO THE BASIC LANGUAGE

BASIC appeared on the scene in 1964, as a simpler language to learn than FORTRAN (which was very popular for mathematical and scientific programming) but with the intention of providing an introduction for programmers who would subsequently learn to program their major projects

WHAT IS A COMPUTER PROGRAM?

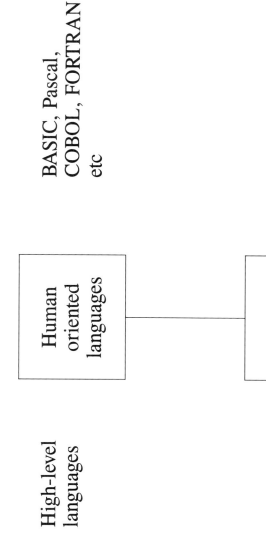

Figure 1.1 Computer Languages Form a Hierarchy

in FORTRAN. As a result, early BASICs were highly mathematical in their orientation, and a large amount of introductory material for the teaching of programming in BASIC is mathematically oriented, even today. However, BASIC has evolved in recent years to become a general-purpose computer language, equally able to cope with Data Processing tasks as with mathematical formulae. Figure 1.2 shows some of the most important high-level languages in their chronological positions.

BASIC has had rather a hard time in recent years and has come under considerable criticism. One of the main reasons for the criticisms is that the language is often used by beginners with no previous programming experience. In addition it does not always encourage the well-structured solutions to problems which are favoured by today's programmers. To criticise the language in this way is rather unfair, since twenty years ago, when the language was first being developed, structured programming techniques had not been invented.

BASIC has reacted to the needs of modern techniques by introducing facilities to allow for better structuring in many of its versions, and to compare it with languages like Pascal which were specifically designed to suit structured programming practices is unfair. The fact that the facilities which caused people to write poor programs have been retained, in order to maintain consistency with earlier BASICs, should hardly be seen as a fault in the language. It is up to the craftsman to see that tools are used to the best possible effect.

A much more legitimate criticism of BASIC is that for reasons of its evolutionary background it has been developed by different manufacturers in different ways, but along broadly similar lines. It is therefore not possible to present a detailed and clear statement of a complete set of instructions which will work satisfactorily on all available BASICs. However, this should be seen as an inconvenience rather than as an insuperable problem.

We shall discuss many techniques which relate to programming in any 'dialect' of BASIC, and then show how these techniques apply in two specific dialects. The reader will find that, equipped with a reference guide for an alternative version of BASIC, simple modifications to the programs developed here will be effective for the system in use.

The lack of standardisation identified here is an argument commonly used in support of languages such as Pascal, which conform rigidly to an International Standard specification, and therefore, in theory, should not suffer from these inconsistencies. Unfortunately, in recent years, hardware advances have encouraged manufacturers to offer 'extended' versions of Pascal. Greater standardisation certainly exists between dialects in Pascal than those of BASIC. However, it is not possible to present a single universally applicable set of instructions for this language either.

Early computers	Programmed in machine code	
First high-level languages	FORTRAN, COBOL, ALGOL60	1960
	BASIC ALGOL68	1970
	Pascal, Prolog	1980
	Ada, Modula 2	

Figure 1.2 Historical Appearance of Programming Languages

COMPUTER PROGRAMS

In order to understand what we are doing when we write a computer program, it is useful to compare the situation with teaching a child how to do something new. Our task is, in that case, to indicate what the child must do in terms of instructions which are already understood. Thus we use a series of instructions which are already within the child's comprehension to describe how to accomplish a new task.

In an analogous way, when we speak of a 'computer program' we are referring to a sequence of instructions written in a computer language, which have been designed in order for the computer to perform a particular task. Thus, we may write a computer program which controls traffic lights at a busy road junction, a computer program which processes examination results, or a computer program which produces gas bills.

In order to write one of these computer programs, we shall need to develop two specific skills.

1 The ability to define a method for solving the problem under consideration.
2 The ability to translate the steps defined in the method into the particular computer language.

Skill 2 indicates the importance of choosing an appropriate language for the solution of a particular problem. When we learn to speak in a foreign language, we can describe anything we wish in any language, providing that we know all the necessary words to make our description and the rules of grammar. Some computer languages do not contain the necessary words to describe certain functions and types of information. It is essential that the particular language chosen contains all the necessary words for the specific application.

An indication of the steps which are involved in progressing from the initial definition of a problem to be solved using a computer, to the completed computer program are illustrated in Figure 1.3.

For some special-purpose applications, the choice of a suitable language becomes crucial. BASIC is a general-purpose computer language and therefore has the advantage that most applications can be adequately described in BASIC. The disadvantage of BASIC is that, for most applications, there would be an alternative, more specialised language which would be better suited, and which would provide a simpler or more appropriate medium to give the description.

Different books vary in their approach to the two specific skills to be presented: some concentrate on presenting the definitions of the language instructions to the exclusion of any instruction in problem-solving methods — we shall refer to these books as **programmers' reference** books. Others begin by presenting programming methodologies and then introduce the language facilities in a traditional and logical order — we shall refer to these as

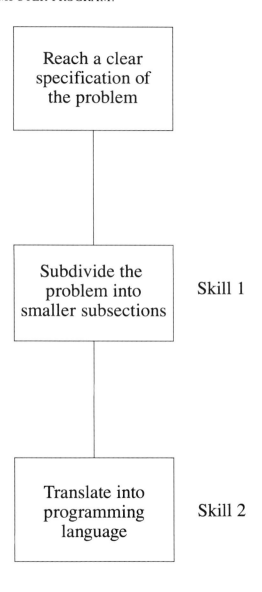

Figure 1.3 Three Stages in Writing a Computer Program

problem-solving guides. Both of these approaches have value: the *programmers' reference* guides are particularly valuable to experienced programmers who are learning to use a new language, while *problem-solving* guides are ideal for those who have some understanding of programming and need to put their informal understanding onto a more formal footing.

In this volume, we do not follow either of these two approaches but instead introduce a series of ideas, each motivated by a desire to tackle a particular programming problem. The programming language's facilities are introduced in an order which is broadly similar to that traditionally used, and problem-solving methods are discussed, but these topics arise naturally from a series of examples which have been chosen because they both are interesting and illustrate techniques in a useful manner. This method has been found to be particularly suited to the complete beginner who has no appreciation of what is involved in programming, and also in 'rescuing' those who have previously tried a more traditional programming course and found it unsatisfactory in some way. The intention in this approach is that even those with no previous experience should rapidly become familiar with computer programs which can accomplish a variety of useful tasks. There is the additional benefit that, once introduced to the instructions used in a few well-written programs which accomplish useful goals, it is often possible for even the complete beginner to adapt the methods used to suit a new but similar situation.

This approach makes it necessary to stress the importance of following the presentation throughout the book in the order in which it is given. Topics and programs discussed in one chapter will be used again in subsequent chapters without any further explanation. Exercises listed at the end of the chapters are designed to be *possible* while using programming techniques which have been covered in the preceding pages. It will not *always* be possible to produce the *most satisfactory* program until later ideas have been assimilated.

The examples given in the text refer to two versions of BASIC: RM BASIC and IBM BASICA (GW BASIC and Turbo Basic are compatible with BASICA). The intention is that, by selecting specific BASIC implementations for the examples, the different facilities within the overall common BASIC language will become apparent. Thus the programmer will become familiar with using alternative strategies dictated by the language differences to achieve the same outcome. Most modern BASICs provide a comparable range of facilities, and this text could be used for programming in these alternative dialects.

COMPUTER CONCEPTS

We have already introduced the idea of a computer program written in a high-level language, such as BASIC. It is appropriate before we begin to write our first program to introduce a number of concepts related to the operation of computer hardware so that the reader will quickly become familiar with the

WHAT IS A COMPUTER PROGRAM? 9

terminology and the significance of some of the basic processes involved.

Acclimatisation

Before you begin, you will need to become familiar with the **hardware configuration.** This simply means that you must begin by finding out a little about the computer you will be using. Typically, you will have several separate boxes which contain a:

— keyboard;
— monitor (screen);
— processor (this will be inside one of the boxes, but you will probably be unable to see it!);
— disk drive(s) (it is possible that you will be sharing a central disk drive, in which case you will not have one of these on your own computer);
— printer (again, you may be sharing a printer with other computer users, in which case you will not have one of these next to you).

Note: you will not necessarily find that each of these occupies a separate box (see Figure 1.4).

You should now become familiar with how to turn on this equipment. It is likely that each separate component of the hardware will have independent power supplies needing up to two switches to be operated before they have been turned on. Furthermore, there is often a requirement that the separate components have to be turned on and off in a particular sequence.

Apart from turning the power on and off, there is likely to be a series of further operations which must be undertaken to make the computer ready for use: these might include (depending on the hardware configuration in use) loading particular disks into disk drives, typing particular instructions on the keyboard and/or giving user names and passwords. A further series of commands is likely to be necessary at the end of a session as a prelude to turning the computer off. You must be sure to become familiar with all these operations, which can take some practice, *before* you attempt to begin to program. Too many people give up learning to program because they feel intimidated by using the equipment and never really feel at home with it. It is the responsibility of every beginner and their tutors to ensure that problems with learning to program really are just that.

Translation

Once the computer is turned on and the necessary version of BASIC is loaded, the computer is ready for use in learning to program. You will recall in our earlier discussion about low-level and high-level languages how instructions written in a high-level language such as BASIC require translation before they

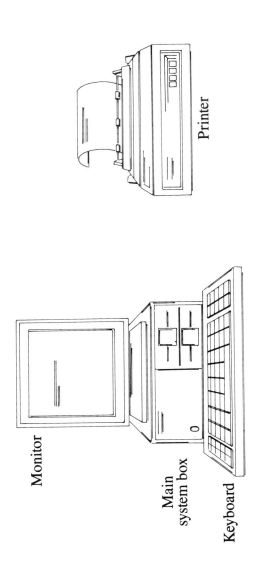

Figure 1.4 The Typical Modern Personal Computer has the Processor and Disk Drives in a Single Box

can be run. There are two principal methods for this translation: the more common of the two, at least where BASIC is concerned, is called **interpretation.**

When a language interpreter is used, each language instruction is translated in turn and immediately executed by the computer. This can allow the manufacturer of a computer to install a particular high-level language into a relatively small area of the computer's memory and is therefore the favoured method for most small microcomputers, where space is particularly tight.

The alternative to interpretation is known as **compilation.** A language compiler translates the entire program, instruction by instruction, before the execution phase is begun. Thus, with a compiler, the so-called 'object code' (ie the translated version of the program) has to be stored in addition to the original program instructions (the 'source code').

There are several advantages in compilation over interpretation, particularly the execution speed of compiled programs, which is substantially higher, and the facility of most compilers to identify all errors of syntax (grammar) by the programmer before execution begins. On the other hand, there are some advantages in interpretation over compilation — particularly for the beginner programmer. These may include the facility to make simple programs run with fewer instructions needing to be learnt or the possibility of running the first part of a longer program, even when it contains errors in syntax later. There is also the likelihood of having an integrated programming environment which permits programs to be run, and disk and printer handling instructions to be given from within the editor. The accurate and efficient identification and correction of errors is also often more easily accomplished with an interpreter (see Figure 1.5).

The Editor

In order to type a computer program into a computer, we shall need to use an **editor**. The editor allows us to type our program instructions into the computer and stores them ready for us to 'run' the program later. In most versions of BASIC, the editor is built into the BASIC system and it is therefore possible simply to type in the program instructions directly. Any compiled BASIC is likely to differ from this: in the case of compiled BASICs (such as Turbo Basic, for example) the editor will be completely separate from the language itself and will be invoked by a separate command. It will also be necessary to exit from the editor before the program is compiled.

Most programming editors allow easy correction of spelling mistakes and easy insertion of extra program lines. Editors fall broadly into two categories: the *screen editor* where corrections are made by moving the cursor to the relevant place and changing the physical appearance of the program on the screen, and the *line editor* which allows modification only to the currently selected line.

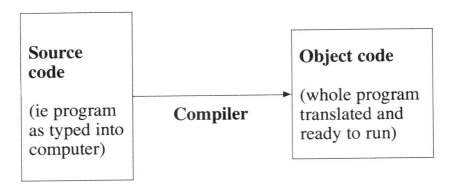

A compiler translates the whole program in readiness for execution

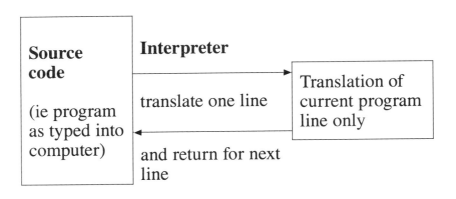

An interpreter translates program one line at a time and this is executed before translating the next line

Figure 1.5   Compilers and Interpreters

WHAT IS A COMPUTER PROGRAM?

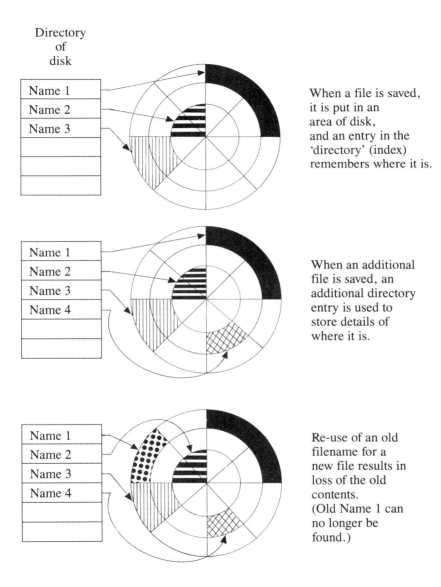

Figure 1.6 Re-use of the Same Filename Results in Loss of the Old File

Either type of editor is quite satisfactory, but each requires some practice.

Saving of Files

One of the most important things to learn about any computer system is how to save the work already typed in so that it can be retrieved next time without retyping. It is characteristic of modern microcomputers that unless the text is *saved*, all the words typed in are lost every time the power is switched off. The most common way to save typing for a future occasion is to save it onto a 'file' on a disk. You will need to learn how to do this, but essentially it is easy. The most important thing to remember is that you will need to give each file of typing a different name, so that when you want to retrieve it you can refer to it by its name. It is particularly important to ensure that you do not re-use the same name for a second file. If you do this, the contents of the earlier file on the disk will be lost as they will be overwritten by the new file (see Figure 1.6).

DON'T PANIC!

This is the end of the introductory chapter, and there is a lot of information in it. Don't worry if you haven't absorbed it all yet. Go on to Chapter 2 and use Chapter 1 for reference as necessary.

2 A First Program

INTRODUCTION

In Chapter 1 we have already identified the importance both of learning a programming language and of developing problem-solving skills. In these early chapters, we shall be concentrating our attentions on the learning of the language; the problem-solving arises later.

In this chapter we meet the following BASIC key words:

(RM BASIC)	(IBM BASICA)
CLS	CLS
HOME	INPUT
INPUT	LIST
LIST	NEW
NEW	PRINT
PRINT	REM
REM	RUN
RUN	

Figure 2.1

BACKGROUND

As an initial example, we will issue some instructions to the computer which cause it to write some words on the computer screen. We shall then learn how to tidy up the screen display.

The first instruction which we meet is the PRINT instruction. The command:

> PRINT "HELLO"

would be interpreted by the computer as meaning that the word HELLO should be displayed on the screen. Similarly,

> PRINT "GO HOME"

would result in the words GO HOME appearing on the screen.

However, we should not think of these single instructions in isolation: in some implementations of BASIC we could type in a single command and get an immediate response from the computer, while in others we could not. Instead we shall form these instructions into a program. To do this, BASIC requires that each instruction should be preceded by a *line number* and, by convention, we number the lines in steps of 10 (ie 10, 20, 30, etc).

Thus a suitable simple program might look like this:

Program 2.1
```
10  PRINT "HELLO"
20  PRINT "I AM YOUR FRIENDLY COMPUTER"
```
Try typing this into the computer and running it. You may need to refer to your instruction manual to find out exactly what to do, but usually you need to begin by typing the word 'NEW'. The command 'NEW' is taken by the computer as an instruction to clear the memory of any previous contents before beginning a new program. This is particularly important if somebody else has been running a program on the same computer before you, since then a failure to type 'NEW' would result in your program instructions becoming superimposed on your predecessor's.

After typing 'NEW', copy the program in, character by character, being careful to reproduce the layout, spelling and punctuation accurately. Press the RETURN or ENTER key at the end of each line. When you have finished typing in the program, type 'RUN' and press RETURN/ENTER, and the program should be executed and behave as we have predicted.

Note: users of Turbo Basic are working in an *'integrated compiler environment'* which means that the editor and command menu system are separate. You will need to ESCAPE from the editor and press 'R' to run the program.

It is possible that you may have made a simple typing error when copying the program in. If so, then depending on precisely what error you made, the program may not run. Execution may stop, and an error message appear on the screen. If this happens, you will need to have a look at the whole program and examine it carefully for errors. Most BASICs highlight whereabouts the error seems to be, but you should not rely on them necessarily being correct every time. It is possible that an error will only become apparent to the computer some time after it occurs — so it is fairly safe to suppose that the error *will not* be further on in the program than the marked position.

In order to look at the program, you may type LIST (or enter the editor mode in Turbo Basic). Now the editor can be used to correct the error before you try to re-run the program.

A FIRST PROGRAM

Upper or Lower Case?

You will have noticed that all the instructions to the computer used so far have been given in upper case (capitals). This is the conventional way of putting in BASIC programs and is compulsory in some implementations. More modern computers are often tolerant of upper or lower case. In this situation, it is probably preferable to use lower case, since words written entirely in upper case characters are more difficult to read quickly, and this discourages visual checks for accuracy of typing, but in order to make instructions stand out in the text, we shall continue to use upper case for some of the examples.

Bugs

Errors in computer programs are often referred to as '**bugs**'. Bugs creep into computer programs in a number of different ways. As we have already remarked, one common cause of bugs is elementary typing errors. This kind of bug is usually easy to find and cure.

A much more serious type of bug arises when a program apparently executes successfully, but in fact performs a wrong function. This is analogous to using the wrong formula in mathematics, but substituting values that are accurate. Where the method is wrong, but the program accurately reflects this wrong method, we refer to its having a logical error. This type of error is made less likely by producing a well designed program. We shall discuss this in much more detail later.

TIDYING THINGS UP

Our first program is rather inelegant in two ways. Firstly, the program simply begins and ends, without giving any account of what it is doing. Admittedly, its purpose is fairly obvious, but we should not allow the simplicity of the program to justify writing poorly presented code (ie instructions in a computer language).

In order to improve our presentation of the program, we need to introduce the **REMark** statement. In many ways this is the simplest BASIC instruction, because it gives a message to the computer to ignore the contents of the current line. This then enables the programmer to give information about the program without fear of confusing the computer. Thus, it is usual to begin each computer program with a REM statement which gives such details as the program's title, purpose, the date it was developed or changed, and the programmer's name. It is permissible to have several such statements at the beginning of the program and others further on, wherever it becomes desirable to give the reader of the program further information about the program and the method in use.

The second area of inelegance in this program is in the presentation of the output. In using the term output, we refer to anything which the computer produces while executing the program, for example on the screen, or on a printer. The main fault with the current example is that the output appears on the screen in addition to whatever else was there before the program run started. Thus, whether the output appears on the top line of the screen, in the middle, or at the bottom depends entirely on the state of the screen prior to starting the program run. This is undesirable, both because it results in the screen looking cluttered, and because it means that the same program will behave differently on different occasions, according to what has gone before. The last point will make testing for accuracy in more complex programs particularly difficult. We are therefore prompted to 'initialise' the computer screen before we begin producing any output. This initialisation consists of clearing the screen of any previous content, and positioning the output cursor (which marks where the next output will appear) at the top left-hand corner of the screen.

In RM BASIC initialisation requires two commands: CLS clears the screen, while HOME takes the cursor to the top left-hand corner.

In the IBM BASICs, the single command CLS performs both functions. Hence we can see that the following programs give an improved presentation to our initial example:

Program 2.2a RM BASIC
```
10  REM IMPROVED APPEARANCE
20  CLS
30  HOME
40  PRINT "HELLO"
50  PRINT "I AM YOUR FRIENDLY COMPUTER"
```

Program 2.2b IBM BASICA
```
10  REM IMPROVED APPEARANCE
20  CLS
30  PRINT "HELLO"
40  PRINT "I AM YOUR FRIENDLY COMPUTER"
```

Notice how in Programs 2.2a and 2.2b the fundamental program is identical, but the screen formatting commands, CLS/HOME and CLS respectively, must be chosen to suit the version of BASIC in use. This will be a common feature of our examples.

DEVELOPING THE THEME

We now consider the problem of having the computer ask a question, and the user supplying an answer. A program which operates in this manner is described as being '**interactive**' because there is interaction between the user and the computer. Until comparatively recently, few programs were interactive. Most

A FIRST PROGRAM

programs did not ask questions of the user and give a quick response, but today many programs, and certainly almost all of those in use on microcomputers, *are* interactive, and therefore the implementation of interactive programs is important.

Persuading the computer to ask a question is not a problem. A simple PRINT statement such as:

PRINT "What is your name?"

will cause the computer to display the question, but instructing it to expect an answer, and to know what to do with the answer, involves us in using an additional command.

The instruction INPUT instructs the computer to expect an answer to a question, and therefore on encountering the command, the computer will halt and await a response from the user. However, before we can finalise the details of the command we need to consider for a moment the way in which the computer stores information.

In BASIC, the computer expects the information it will need to store to be presented to it in one of two main forms. Either the information consists of a number, or a string of characters (roughly speaking, a word or phrase). The computer is able to reserve boxes to store the information, and each of these boxes is given a name by the programmer. The programmer must instruct the computer as to whether each box created is to be the correct shape for a number, or the correct shape for a string of characters. As a general rule, we must consider the two types of box to be incompatible and not try to store items in the wrong shaped box.

We can only store information in boxes the correct shape (see Figure 2.2). How do we define the shape of a box? Well, in BASIC it is easy, because all the number-shaped boxes have names (identifiers) made up of a letter followed by other letters and numbers — eg FRED, F2E6, JILL78, whereas the string-shaped boxes have similar names but with a dollar sign ($) tacked on the end — eg FRED$, F34$, NF$, etc.

How many of these boxes we are permitted to have at any one time depends upon the amount of memory available for storage. In practice, users of computers today are fairly unlikely to find any constraints on space for storage of simple variables such as those we have described here.

To return to our particular example, we are now in a position to instruct the computer to accept the input of a user's name. From the above discussion, it is obvious that the name will need to be stored in a box referred to by an identifier ending in a dollar sign. It is customary to refer to the information stored by identifiers which in some way describe the information — so it would be appropriate to identify the storage location as NAME$ — this will help us to

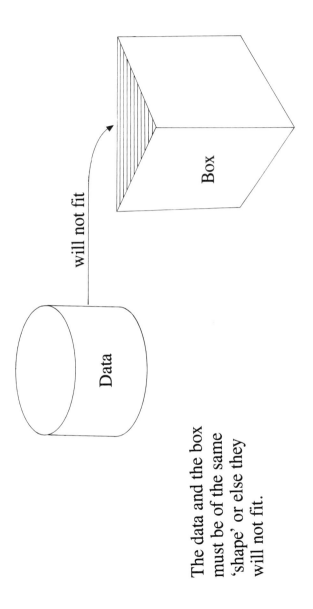

Figure 2.2

The data and the box must be of the same 'shape' or else they will not fit.

A FIRST PROGRAM

keep track of what information it contains.

Programs 2.3a and 2.3b give examples of how the input statement would be used to accept the user's name and store it in the location NAME$.

Program 2.3a RM BASIC

```
10  REM IMPROVED APPEARANCE
20  CLS
30  HOME
40  PRINT "HELLO"
50  PRINT "I AM YOUR FRIENDLY COMPUTER"
60  PRINT "WHAT IS YOUR NAME?"
70  INPUT NAME$
```

Program 2.3b IBM BASICA

```
10  REM IMPROVED APPEARANCE
20  CLS
30  PRINT "HELLO"
40  PRINT "I AM YOUR FRIENDLY COMPUTER"
50  PRINT "WHAT IS YOUR NAME?"
60  INPUT NAME$
```

Note: although we know that the information which will be typed into the computer in response to its question will be the user's name, the computer is not aware of this. It is very easy to lose sight of the fact that the computer is not an intelligent machine (in the human sense) and therefore only does exactly as it is told. Therefore, the computer cannot perform any error checking on the name typed in, and will find '££&!' as equally acceptable as 'Fred Smith'.

In an attempt to distinguish between the information as stored in a computer (which has no appreciation of what it signifies) and the actual meaning which we attach to the information, we shall use the word *'data'* to describe what is stored in the computer with no meaning attached to it, and we shall reserve the term *'information'* to refer to the data together with its meaning. Thus, when we type information into the computer, all the computer sees is data, but the data output by the computer is viewed by us as information!

Having written a program which stores the user's name in the box called NAME$, we had better use it for something. We shall add a further question to the program, so that the computer responds by asking where the user lives. In doing this, we shall use the name which we have already stored, so that the computer asks, 'Where do you live, Sam?' and substitutes the appropriate name in the question.

We can do this by using a slightly more complex version of the print statement:

```
PRINT "Where do you live, ";NAME$
```

Add this statement to your program at the next suitable line-number.

Notice in this print statement how the words 'Where do you live' are enclosed in inverted commas ("), but the word NAME$ is outside the inverted commas. This is because we want the computer to copy out the words 'Where do you live' but *refer back* to find the contents of the box which we have called NAME$. Thus words in print statements which are not enclosed within inverted commas refer to boxes (or variables) by that name.

There are three other technical features of the PRINT statement which we have just described. We shall identify them here, but we will meet them again later, so do not worry if you do not understand them at this stage:

1 The comma is enclosed within the inverted commas. This is because we actually want the comma to be copied out as a part of our output.
2 There is a space after the comma, also enclosed within the inverted commas. This is so that there will be a space between the comma and the person's name.
3 There is a semicolon between the closing inverted commas and the variable name NAME$. This tells the computer to print the name *immediately* after the content of the inverted commas, without leaving any further gap.

You should experiment with these 'formatting' instructions within the print statement. Try, for example, replacing the semicolon with a comma, or removing it altogether. Try removing the space before the closing inverted commas. Finally, try a print statement like this:

PRINT "Where do you come from, "; NAME$;" and how long does it take to get here from your home?"

Notice once again how the semicolons are used to keep the output flowing continuously with no extra gaps and the text to be copied out is held between inverted commas. If we return now to our general discussion of the program, we find the program currently in this form:

Program 2.4a RM BASIC

```
10  REM IMPROVED APPEARANCE
20  CLS
30  HOME
40  PRINT "HELLO"
50  PRINT "I AM YOUR FRIENDLY COMPUTER"
60  PRINT "WHAT IS YOUR NAME?"
70  INPUT NAME$
80  PRINT "WHERE DO YOU COME FROM ";NAME$;"?"
```

A FIRST PROGRAM

Program 2.4b IBM BASICA
```
10  REM IMPROVED APPEARANCE
20  CLS
30  PRINT "HELLO"
40  PRINT "I AM YOUR FRIENDLY COMPUTER"
50  PRINT "WHAT IS YOUR NAME?"
60  INPUT NAME$
70  PRINT "WHERE DO YOU COME FROM ";NAME$;"?"
```
The additional "?" has been added to complete the final question.

Notice that the computer is at present finishing the program run by asking a question, but it has not yet been instructed to expect an answer to the question. In order to teach it to expect an answer, it will require an INPUT statement and a suitable box name (variable) will have to be defined.

Exercise A

As a short exercise, Figure 2.3 shows a series of questions and answers on a computer screen. Extend your program so that the computer conducts the same conversation with the user as illustrated in Figure 2.3. A suitable program is listed in Appendix 3 as Programs 2.5a and b.

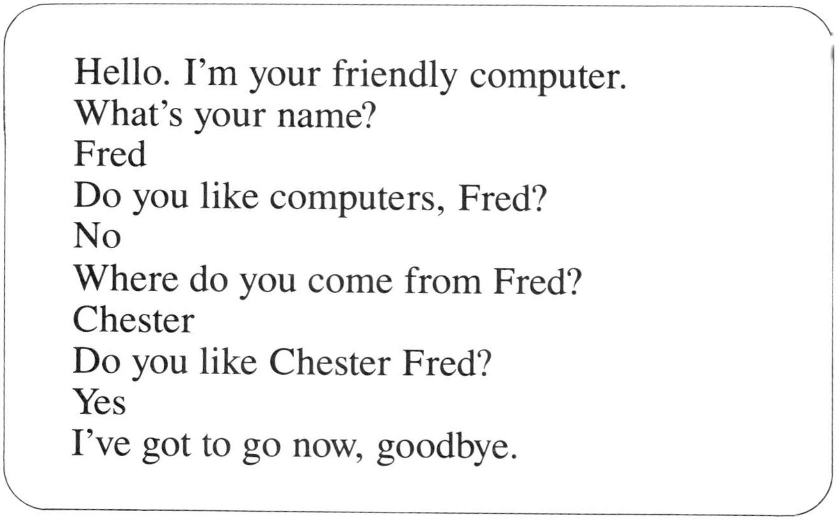

Hello. I'm your friendly computer.
What's your name?
Fred
Do you like computers, Fred?
No
Where do you come from Fred?
Chester
Do you like Chester Fred?
Yes
I've got to go now, goodbye.

Figure 2.3 Computer Screen in a Simple Interactive Session

> ## VAT Analysis
>
> This program accepts details of the total amount spent (net of tax) and the % tax payable. It then displays the amount of tax due.
>
> Please type in the amount spent in £
> 250
> Please type in the VAT rate (%)
> 10
> Total tax payable is £25

Figure 2.4 Computer Screen Appearance for Simple Tax Calculation Program

ELEMENTARY CALCULATIONS

Simple calculations based on the numerical values of numerical variables (boxes designed to take in numbers), are so simple that no description is offered at this stage, but an example is presented in Program 2.6.

Program 2.6

```
10   REM PROGRAM TO CALCULATE THE AVERAGE OF
     3 NUMBERS
20   PRINT "THIS PROGRAM ASKS FOR MARKS OUT OF
     100 FOR 3 EXAMS"
30   PRINT "TYPE IN MARK FOR MATHS"
40   INPUT MATHS
50   PRINT "TYPE IN MARK FOR FRENCH"
60   INPUT FRENCH
70   PRINT "TYPE IN MARK FOR CHEMISTRY"
80   INPUT CHEM
90   SUMMARK=MATHS+FRENCH+CHEM
100  AVEMARK = SUMMARK/3
120  PRINT "AVERAGE MARK IS ";AVEMARK
```

A FIRST PROGRAM

Exercise B

Program 2.6 is independent of any specific version of BASIC because it does not use the types of language features which are dependent upon the hardware. The presentation of the program is correspondingly poor. Rewrite the program with simple additions to improve screen presentation.

Exercise C

Figure 2.4 displays the screen when a particular program is run. Write a suitable program. (A solution will be found in Appendix 3, Program 2.7.)

SUMMARY

In this chapter, we have met some simple computer programs. These programs have illustrated methods for putting information of two types — numerical and string — into the computer and some simple output formatting techniques. Some simple numerical calculations have also been introduced.

3 Improve Your Presentation

INTRODUCTION

In Chapter 2 we met very elementary techniques for improving the appearance of output on the screen from simple computer programs. Modern computer hardware is frequently capable of producing some very impressive graphical images using colour and text, which can be very effective and programmed comparatively easily. In this chapter we shall be investigating some of these slightly more advanced display handling facilities, which we shall then be able to use to good effect later in our programming. The techniques introduced are all very simple to use, and rely heavily on today's advanced computer technology. Even a very few years ago, such graphical images would have been significantly more difficult to program in BASIC.

The most noticeable problem which we shall face in utilising graphical facilities on the computer is the non-standard nature of the commands which must be used to obtain the desired results. Thus, in this chapter more than elsewhere, a large proportion of the text is machine specific, and users of alternative hardware and different implementations of BASIC are more likely to need to refer to reference manuals to discover comparable techniques.

GRAPHICS SCREEN LAYOUT

The graphics screen of the computer is laid out as though it were a piece of graph paper and co-ordinates are used to describe different screen locations. On most computers there is a trade-off between 'resolution' of the screen (ie how 'sharp' the image is) and the number of different colours available at any given moment. Naturally these two issues are also heavily dependent on the hardware in use. Different options available for a particular hardware configuration are known as the **'graphics modes'**. Figure 3.1a shows the two RM BASIC graphics modes, and Figure 3.1b shows two of the available graphics screen modes for IBM BASICA, with a colour graphics adapter.

RM BASIC Mode 40

RM BASIC Mode 80

Figure 3.1a

IMPROVE YOUR PRESENTATION

IBM BASICA Screen 1

IBM BASICA Screen 2

Figure 3.1b

DRAWING SOME SIMPLE SHAPES
RM BASIC

RM BASIC has a statement SET MODE to initialise a particular graphics mode. So, for example, the statement SET MODE 40 or SET MODE 80 selects between low resolution 16-colour graphics and high resolution 4-colour graphics respectively.

The command SET PAPER n (where n is a number between 0 and 3 for high resolution mode, or a number between 0 and 15 for low resolution mode, followed by a CLS statement) sets a new background colour, while SET BRUSH n selects a colour for drawing. There are also SET PEN n and SET BORDER n to change the colour of the text and the border of the screen respectively. Some simple experimentation will help the programmer to discover the correspondence between numbers and particular colours. One danger which the programmer should have in mind is that if the text and background are inadvertently set to the same colour, then all the writing on the screen will be invisible!

By way of a simple example, we shall use the AREA command to draw a rectangle. (Program 3.1 and Figure 3.2.)

Program 3.1

```
10  REM Simple Drawing Program
20  SET MODE 80
30  SET PAPER 2
40  SET PEN 1
50  SET BRUSH 3
60  CLS: HOME
70  PRINT "This is some writing in colour number 1"
80  AREA 50,50;100,50;100,100;50,100
```

The AREA command is very versatile and allows any polygonal shape (ie any shape which is made up of simple straight line edges) to be drawn and shaded-in using the current brush colour. In this way, squares, rectangles, pentagons, triangles, and so on can be made using the same command. All that is necessary is to give the command AREA followed by the required list of co-ordinate pairs, separated by semicolons as in this example.

The one cautionary note about the use of the AREA command is to ensure that the vertices (corners) are listed in the correct order, because the straight lines are drawn in the order in which the co-ordinates are listed. If the co-ordinates are listed in the wrong order, rectangles become egg-timer shapes and some very unusual results may be obtained.

The CIRCLE command is also very easy to use. The command CIRCLE

IMPROVE YOUR PRESENTATION

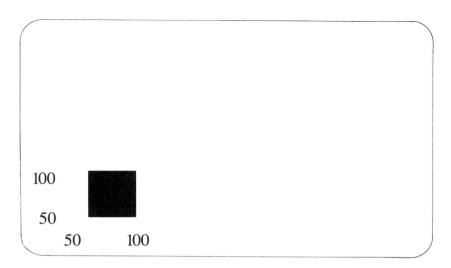

Figure 3.2   The Appearance of the Screen After Running Program 3.1
(Note that co-ordinates are given for guidance only.)

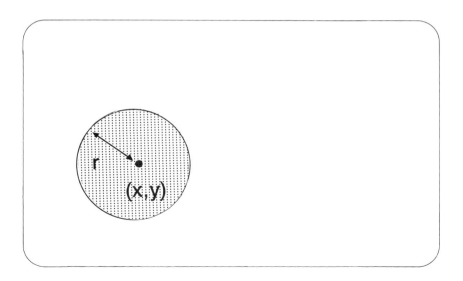

Figure 3.3   CIRCLE r,x,y Draws a Circle of Radius r at Centre x,y

r, x, y draws a circle of radius r units centred at x, y. The circle is shaded-in using the current brush colour. (See Figure 3.3.)

You will not be warned if part or all of your image is not within the limits on the screen. Therefore it is often the case that something may go missing because the co-ordinates are out of range. This facility can be used to draw a circle near the screen's edge, so that only a semicircle appears.

It is very good practice at experimental programming to design some displays and to try to implement them by writing simple programs. Try making a picture of a rainbow by superimposing circles of different colours, or of a windmill. How about a picture of Mickey Mouse!?

Finally, text can be positioned on the graphics screen in two ways. Normal size text can be printed as usual, but it is often easier to use the alternative PLOT command.

The command:

$$\text{PLOT ``Hello'',x, y}$$

causes the word "Hello" to appear in the current brush colour with the bottom left-hand corner of H at the co-ordinate point x, y. When the PLOT command is used in place of PRINT, there is the added facility to change the size of the text which appears on the screen. This is done by the use of the command SET PLOT SIZE n where n is 1, 2, 3, 4 or 5. The text size in subsequent PLOT commands, is the normal size multiplied by the factor n. The example below would cause 'Hello' to be printed in large letters starting at the point 100,100. (See Program 3.2 and Figure 3.4.)

Program 3.2

```
10  REM Big print
20  SET PLOT SIZE 3
30  PLOT "Hello", 100,100
```

Exercise A

Write a program which reproduces the screen display illustrated in Figure 3.5.

MOVING PRINT AND INPUT AROUND THE SCREEN

The PLOT command is best suited to outputting text from within a graphics program, but it may be necessary at times to move text, output by the PRINT statement, to a particular screen location, or (more commonly) to accept data typed in to an INPUT statement at an appropriate position. In order to do this, RM BASIC provides a SET CURPOS command, which moves the text cursor to a particular screen location. Thus, the commands:

(100,100)

Figure 3.4 (The co-ordinates are shown for convenience.)

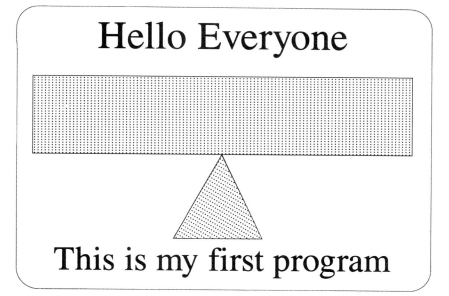

Figure 3.5

```
SET CURPOS 15,20
INPUT FRED
```
will cause the number, to be stored as FRED, to be typed in at a prompt at screen location 15,20. Unfortunately, the text co-ordinates used by SET CURPOS do not use the same grid references as the graphics co-ordinates already described. Text co-ordinates vary horizontally between 1 and 80 (or 40 according to the screen mode), and vertically between 1 and 25 (1 being at the *top* of the screen and 25 at the *bottom*). (See Figure 3.6.)

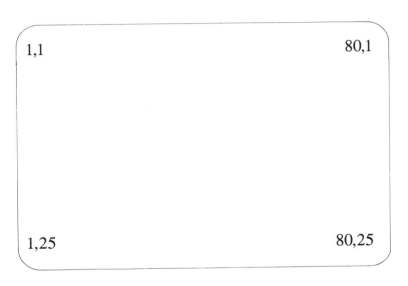

Figure 3.6 Text Screen Co-ordinates in Mode 80

Note: in common with other modern versions of the BASIC language, RM BASIC contains a wide range of simple graphics instructions to provide a variety of facilities for the user. It is not the purpose of this book to introduce all the facilities, which could be easily found in the Reference Manual. We have, instead, concentrated on introducing a few techniques which will be generally applicable in developing attractive screen presentations and suggesting when they might be appropriate.

IBM BASICA

In order to use the graphics facilities of IBM BASICA, a SCREEN command

IMPROVE YOUR PRESENTATION

must be issued. The facilities available are determined by the precise hardware configuration in use, and in particular on the type of display adapter/monitor combination installed. The two possible modes which we shall discuss here are modes 1 and 2 since these are supported on almost all common hardware, and they provide simple graphics facilities. Higher resolution, and more colours, are provided by other modes, but they are available only on a restricted set of hardware.

The command:

SCREEN 1

sets the display to 40 column mode, medium resolution graphics (see Figure 3.1b(i)).

The command:

SCREEN 2

sets the display to 80 column width and high resolution graphics (see Figure 3.1b(ii)). Either of these screen commands also clears the screen of its current contents.

As a first example, we shall draw and shade-in a rectangular box on the screen. This will require the use of the LINE command to draw the box, and the PAINT command to shade it in. Figure 3.7 shows the co-ordinates referenced in the program listed below (Program 3.3).

Program 3.3

```
10  REM Box drawing
20  SCREEN 1
30  LINE (50,50) −(100,50),2
40  LINE −(100,100),2
50  LINE −(100,50),2
60  LINE −(50,50),2
70  PAINT −(75,75),2
```

In this program, two alternative forms of the LINE instruction are used. In line 30, two points (50,50) and (100,50) are given. This instruction causes a line to be drawn joining the two points. In subsequent LINE instructions, only the destination of the line need be given, and the computer automatically starts the new line from the end of the previous one. If a second separate shape was required, then a further instruction of the form of line 30 would be used to provide a new starting point. The second feature of the instruction LINE, is the appearance of the ',2' at the end of each instruction. The ',2' defines the colour for drawing each of the lines.

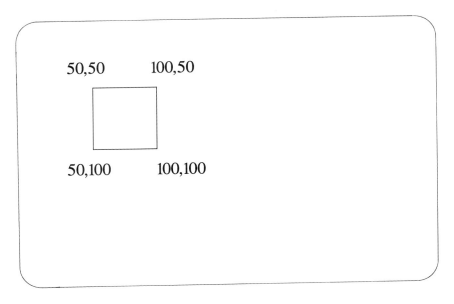

Figure 3.7 Screen Appearance When Program 3.3 is Run

Exercise B

Experiment with alternative numbers replacing the colour 2, and draw up a list of numbers and their corresponding colours. You will discover that the higher resolution mode offers a more restricted choice of colours.

The PAINT instruction contains co-ordinates and a colour selection. The co-ordinates define any single point in the interior of an enclosed region on the screen. This region is then PAINTed in the colour given by the final number in the instruction (Figure 3.8). Note that the boundary of the region must be drawn in the same colour as the region will be painted.

The command CIRCLE (x, y), r, c draws the outline of a circle centred at (x, y) with radius r in colour c. (See Figure 3.9.) The PAINT instruction can be used again to shade in the circle. Only those parts of a circle which lie within the screen co-ordinate range will be displayed, and so it is possible to produce, for example, semicircles centred at the edge of the screen.

Experimentation with the CIRCLE, LINE and PAINT commands is an interesting and useful exercise, although the range of colours available on many IBM-compatible computers is disappointing. Try to make some simple and effective screen displays; for example, a windmill, the Olympic logo, or a

IMPROVE YOUR PRESENTATION

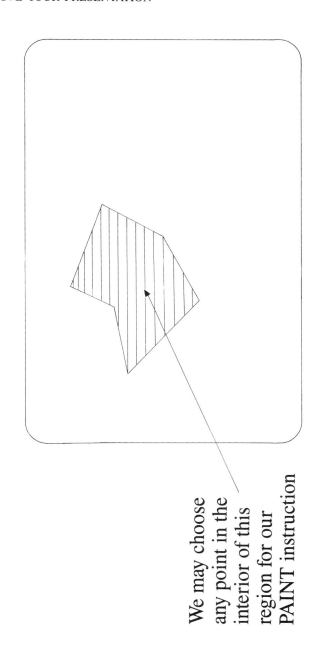

Figure 3.8 Co-ordinates in the PAINT Instruction

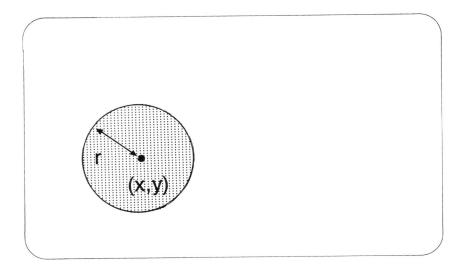

Figure 3.9 The Command CIRCLE (x,y),r,c Draws a Circle, Centre (x,y) Radius r in Colour c

drawing of Mickey Mouse!

In order to incorporate text into a graphics display or, indeed, in order to locate text in a specific place on the computer screen, we shall require the command LOCATE. Unfortunately, LOCATE requires us to use text, rather than graphics co-ordinates, and therefore we must simultaneously have in mind two alternative co-ordinate systems which are used to describe screen locations. We can see how this works out in 40-column mode in Figure 3.10.

Figure 3.11 shows how the horizontal graphics co-ordinates from 0 to 319 along the x-axis correspond to text co-ordinates from 1 to 40, 8 graphics pixels (picture cells) corresponding to a single character cell. Similarly, vertical graphics co-ordinates numbered from 0 to 199 correspond to text co-ordinates in the range 1 to 25.

Note: it is important to remember that the vertical co-ordinate systems increase as one moves *down* the screen and not in the mathematical sense of the y-axis increasing vertically upwards.

The method of displaying text on the screen in a particular location now consists of the two commands:

IMPROVE YOUR PRESENTATION   39

Figure 3.10 Text Screen Co-ordinates 40 Column Mode

LOCATE (x, y)
PRINT "Hello"

and it is often convenient to include them in a single program line as:

LOCATE (x, y) : PRINT "Hello"

In this case, the use of the colon (:) to separate the two instructions is essential.

Exercise C

Reproduce the screen display from Figure 3.12 in a program.

INPUT AND OUTPUT

In our discussion of presentation so far, we have been considering methods of improving the screen display of what we might describe as *static* (or *fixed*) *components*. By this term we mean those items displayed on the computer screen which are predetermined when the program is first written. However, this is not really sufficient, since we may wish to have screen output which relates to previous inputs (and is therefore dynamic) and still wish to have full control of the screen's appearance in this situation. Programs which approximate the screen shown in Figure 3.13 appear as Programs 3.4a and 3.4b.

40 BASIC APPLICATIONS

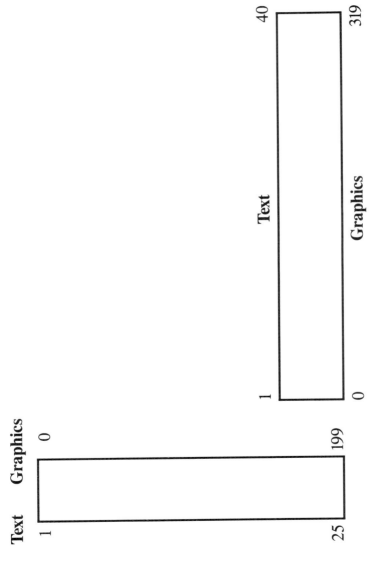

Figure 3.11 Rulers Indicate Correspondence between Text and Graphics Co-ordinate Systems

Hello Everyone

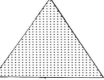

This is my first program

Figure 3.12

Hello, what's your name?
John
Do you like it here, John?

Figure 3.13 An Interactive Display

Program 3.4a (RM BASIC)

```
10  REM Question and answer
20  SET MODE 80
30  CLS:HOME
40  SET PLOT SIZE 2
50  PLOT "Hello, what's your name?",100,200
60  SET CURPOS 15,6
70  INPUT Name$
80  PLOT "Do you like it here, "+ Name$,100,100
```

Program 3.4b (IBM Version)

```
10  REM Question and answer
20  SCREEN 2
30  CLS
40  LOCATE 10,3
50  PRINT "Hello, what's your name?"
60  LOCATE 10,5
70  INPUT Name$
80  LOCATE 10,7
90  PRINT "Do you like it here, "; Name$
```

Remark: the situation in the IBM BASICA example is slightly simpler and does not require concatenation (addition) of strings. However, the level of programmer control over the appearance of the output is much greater with RM BASIC, where the size of the text and the position can be controlled by the programmer. The greater range of facilities on offer brings with it the need to understand a wider range of commands. It would have been possible to use SET CURPOS and PRINT in place of PLOT, in the RM BASIC example, if the inferior screen presentation was acceptable.

Exercise D

Design a display (using graph paper) integrating text and graphics which can be used as a 'Title Page' to your overall piece of work in BASIC. It should incorporate your name, and the words 'BASIC Programming' and the date. When you are satisfied with the design on paper, write a program which will reproduce your design on the computer screen.

Exercise E

Presentation of computer software (programs) is becoming increasingly important as users are becoming more experienced and demand more attractive screen layouts. Design a question and answer program with a series of questions, and try several alternative screen layouts. (In some, you might vary the positions of the questions on the screen, with others, you might clear the screen after every question or two, while with some more, you might incorporate graphics images or logos within your screens.) When you have several alternatives, ask someone else to try them out, and to tell you which layouts are the most attractive to the user.

A REAL APPLICATION

Our first really significant programming example is drawn from education for the very young, and the need to teach children about colour and shape. We shall produce a **menu-driven** program which allows a teacher or child to select a particular shape and colour, and produce a display on the computer screen of the required shape in the specified colour.

This example introduces the concept of menu-driven programs as well as utilising both simple selection techniques and **procedures** to produce a well-**structured** program. We discuss structure and procedures more formally in later chapters, but the aim here is to break the problem down into manageable units before programming.

The program will utilise three separate screen displays, illustrated in Figure 3.14. The first screen presents a menu offering a choice of colour, the second offers a similar menu to choose a shape. The third screen utilises the selections on the earlier screen to produce the required output.

The program will be written in three sections, each section corresponding to one of the screens seen when the program is run and we shall call the three sections of code MENU1, MENU2, and OUTPUT.

Here we will describe the development of the complete program. It is important to remember that programs are best developed on a piece of rough paper, and then gradually rewritten into a neat (and complete) version, before typing them into the computer. In particular, it is often appropriate to omit line numbers when the program is developed on paper and insert them later.

In Program 3.5 some BASIC code (program instructions) are presented which will produce MENU1 on the screen. Notice how the chosen colour is stored in a variable CLOR.

Program 3.5 RM BASIC version

(The IBM version is identical except for the omission of the HOME instruction.)

```
REM MENU1
CLS
HOME
PRINT
PRINT "SELECT COLOUR OF CHOICE"
PRINT
PRINT "1. GREEN"
```

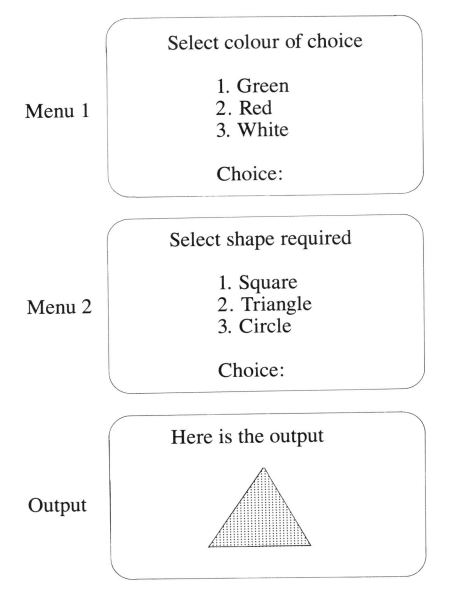

Figure 3.14   Three Screen Displays Within the Current Example Program

```
    PRINT
    PRINT "2. RED"
    PRINT
    PRINT "3. WHITE"
    PRINT
    PRINT "Type in selection"
    INPUT CLOR
```

Exercise F

Write a rough draft of the corresponding BASIC statements to produce MENU2 and store the selection in a variable called SHAPE. (A suitable program segment is given in Appendix 3, Program 3.6.)

The final section of the program, which we have called OUTPUT, is the most complicated. Figure 3.15 gives a tree diagram which shows the various options available and the expected outcomes. Suitable program statements to accomplish this are shown in Programs 3.7a, b and c.

Program 3.7a

RM BASIC version of OUTPUT

```
    IF SHAPE=1 THEN Drawsquare ELSE IF SHAPE=2 THEN Drawcircle
    ELSE Drawtriangle
```

Program 3.7b

Turbo Basic version of OUTPUT

```
    IF SHAPE=1 THEN CALL DRAWSQUARE ELSE IF SHAPE=2 THEN
    CALL DRAWCIRCLE ELSE CALL DRAWTRIANGLE
```

Program 3.7c

IBM BASICA version of OUTPUT

```
    IF SHAPE=1 THEN GOSUB 4000:REM DRAWSQUARE
    IF SHAPE=2 THEN GOSUB 5000:REM DRAWCIRCLE
    IF SHAPE=3 THEN GOSUB 6000:REM DRAWTRIANGLE
```

Notice how, in Programs 3.7a, b and c, the IF statement is used to decide which shape has been selected, another procedure is then called to actually draw the shape. We therefore still have to write three further sections of program to select the colour and actually draw the shapes. This is normal practice and makes the OUTPUT routine more readable and more easily designed, since the technical problems of getting the shapes drawn exactly right are left to separate subsections of the program code. We shall leave this detail for the present, and incorporate it into the complete program (which is listed as Program 3.9).

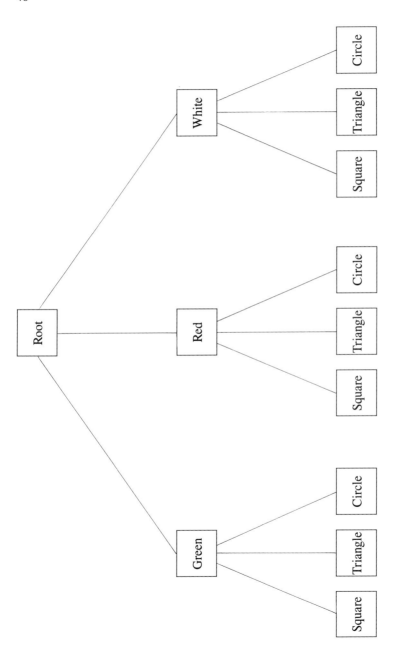

Figure 3.15 Tree Diagram Showing Nine Possible Routes Through Program

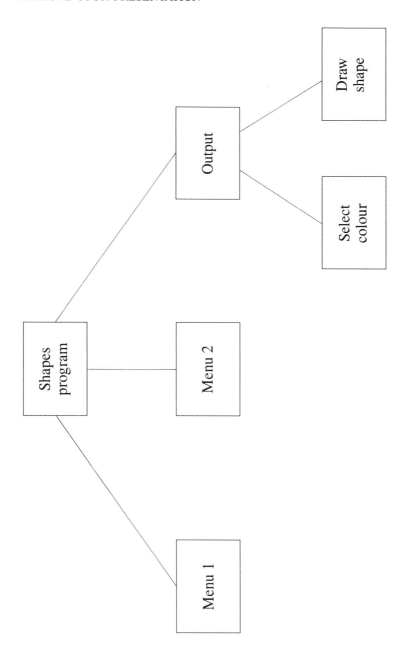

Figure 3.16 Simple Program Structure Diagram

It can be useful to draw a diagram to illustrate the overall structure of the program as we have designed it, and a suitable diagram is shown in Figure 3.16. These diagrams will be discussed in much more detail later, but the present one is included for completeness and for later reference.

We shall now construct the overall program, which is surprisingly simple, and then incorporate the sections of program which we have just written. Remember that the program simply needs to perform three operations in turn and then finish. We have called these three operations MENU1, MENU2 and OUTPUT. The main part of the program is therefore simply this:

Program 3.8a (RM BASIC)

```
10  REM Shape drawing program
20  MENU1
30  MENU2
40  OUTPUT
50  END
```

Program 3.8b (Turbo Basic)

```
10  REM Shape drawing program
20  CALL MENU1
30  CALL MENU2
40  CALL OUTPUT
50  END
```

Program 3.8c (IBM BASICA)

```
10  REM Shape drawing program
20  GOSUB 1000:REM MENU1
30  GOSUB 2000:REM MENU2
40  GOSUB 3000:REM OUTPUT
50  END
```

Note how the program instructions simply list the three section names in the order in which they are to appear.

We must then add to the end of the main program the descriptions of each of the three main subsections, and those of the three subsections used by the OUTPUT section. The complete program is shown in Programs 3.9a, b and c.

Program 3.9a (RM BASIC version)

The complete program

```
10  REM Shape drawing program
15  GLOBAL Shape, Clor
20  MENU1
30  MENU2
```

```
40   OUTPUT
50   END
60   PROCEDURE MENU1
65   GLOBAL Clor
70   CLS
80   HOME
90   PRINT
100  PRINT "SELECT COLOUR OF CHOICE"
110  PRINT
120  PRINT "1. GREEN"
130  PRINT
140  PRINT "2. RED"
150  PRINT
160  PRINT "3. WHITE"
170  PRINT
180  PRINT "Type in selection"
190  INPUT Clor
200  ENDPROC
210  PROCEDURE MENU2
220  GLOBAL Shape
230  CLS
240  HOME
250  PRINT
260  PRINT "SELECT SHAPE OF CHOICE"
270  PRINT
280  PRINT "1. SQUARE"
290  PRINT
300  PRINT "2. CIRCLE"
310  PRINT
320  PRINT "3. TRIANGLE"
330  PRINT
340  PRINT "Type in selection"
350  INPUT Shape
360  ENDPROC
370  PROCEDURE OUTPUT
375  GLOBAL Shape,Clor
380  IF Shape=1 THEN Drawsquare ELSE IF Shape=2 THEN Drawcircle ELSE Drawtriangle
390  ENDPROC
400  PROCEDURE Drawsquare
405  GLOBAL Clor
410  IF Clor=1 THEN SET BRUSH 1 ELSE IF Clor=2 THEN SET BRUSH 2 ELSE SET BRUSH 3
```

```
420  AREA 100,100;200,100;200,200;100,200
430  ENDPROC
440  PROCEDURE Drawcircle
445  GLOBAL Clor
450  IF Clor=1 THEN SET BRUSH 1 ELSE IF Clor=2 THEN
     SET BRUSH 2 ELSE SET BRUSH 3
460  CIRCLE 100,300,150
470  ENDPROC
480  PROCEDURE Drawtriangle
485  GLOBAL Clor
490  IF Clor=1 THEN SET BRUSH 1 ELSE IF Clor=2 THEN
     SET BRUSH 2 ELSE SET BRUSH 3
500  AREA 100,100;500,100;300,225
510  ENDPROC
```

Program 3.9b Turbo Basic version

The complete program

```
 10  REM Shape drawing program
 20  CALL MENU1
 30  CALL MENU2
 40  CALL OUTPUT
 50  END
 60  SUB MENU1
 65  SHARED Clor
 70  CLS
 90  PRINT
100  PRINT "SELECT COLOUR OF CHOICE"
110  PRINT
120  PRINT "1. GREEN"
130  PRINT
140  PRINT "2. RED"
150  PRINT
160  PRINT "3. WHITE"
170  PRINT
180  PRINT "Type in selection"
190  INPUT Clor
200  END SUB
210  SUB MENU2
220  SHARED Shape
230  CLS
250  PRINT
260  PRINT "SELECT SHAPE OF CHOICE"
270  PRINT
```

```
280  PRINT "1. SQUARE"
290  PRINT
300  PRINT "2. CIRCLE"
310  PRINT
320  PRINT "3. TRIANGLE"
330  PRINT
340  PRINT "Type in selection"
350  INPUT Shape
360  END SUB
370  SUB OUTPUT
375  SHARED Clor, Shape
380  IF Shape=1 THEN CALL DRAWSQUARE ELSE
     IF Shape=2 THEN CALL DRAWCIRCLE ELSE CALL
     DRAWTRIANGLE
390  END SUB
400  SUB DRAWSQUARE
405  SHARED Clor
410  LINE (100,100)−(100,200)
420  LINE −(200,200)
430  LINE −(200,100)
440  LINE −(100,100)
450  PAINT (150,150),Clor
460  END SUB
470  SUB DRAWCIRCLE
475  SHARED Clor
480  CIRCLE (150,150),100,Clor
490  END SUB
500  SUB DRAWTRIANGLE
510  SHARED Clor
520  LINE (100,100)−(200,100)
530  LINE −(150,150)
540  LINE −(100,100)
550  PAINT (150,125),Clor
560  END SUB
```

Program 3.9c IBM BASICA version

The complete program

```
10  REM Shape drawing program
20  GOSUB 60 : REM MENU1
30  GOSUB 210 : REM MENU2
40  GOSUB 370 : REM OUTPUT
50  END
60  REM MENU1
```

```
 70  CLS
 90  PRINT
100  PRINT "SELECT COLOUR OF CHOICE"
110  PRINT
120  PRINT "1. GREEN"
130  PRINT
140  PRINT "2. RED"
150  PRINT
160  PRINT "3. WHITE"
170  PRINT
180  PRINT "Type in selection"
190  INPUT Clor
200  RETURN
210  REM MENU2
230  CLS
250  PRINT
260  PRINT "SELECT SHAPE OF CHOICE"
270  PRINT
280  PRINT "1. SQUARE"
290  PRINT
300  PRINT "2. CIRCLE"
310  PRINT
320  PRINT "3. TRIANGLE"
330  PRINT
340  PRINT "Type in selection"
350  INPUT Shape
360  RETURN
370  REM OUTPUT
380  IF Shape=1 THEN GOSUB 400 ELSE IF Shape=2 THEN
     GOSUB 470 ELSE GOSUB 500
390  RETURN
400  REM DRAWSQUARE
410  LINE (100,100)-(100,200)
420  LINE -(200,200)
430  LINE -(200,100)
440  LINE -(100,100)
450  PAINT (150,150),CLOR
460  RETURN
470  REM DRAWCIRCLE
480  CIRCLE (150,150),100,CLOR
490  RETURN
500  REM DRAWTRIANGLE
520  LINE (100,100)-(200,100)
```

```
530   LINE  -(150,150)
540   LINE  -(100,100)
550   PAINT (150,125),CLOR
560   RETURN
```

Look at all three programs listed above and take careful note of the similarity in their design, even where the actual language statements of the three versions of BASIC have dictated a different approach.

Note the use of the words PROCEDURE, SUB and GOSUB respectively to refer to the sections of the program, and END SUB, ENDPROC and RETURN to mark the end of each subsection. These separate sections into which a program is subdivided are termed **procedures**, **subprograms** or **subroutines**. Notice also, that the oldest version of the language (in this case BASICA) does not offer the ability to call *named* procedures, but references must instead be by line-number which is rather less convenient. We may, however, use REM statements as illustrated here to assist with readability. Throughout our discussion, we shall use the term 'procedure' whenever we need to refer to a self-contained section of program. (The addition of the GLOBAL/SHARED statements in the RM BASIC and Turbo Basic programs refers to the way in which values of CLOR and SHAPE are handed from one procedure to another and this is discussed more fully in later chapters.)

Exercise G

Adapt the program given in Programs 3.9a, b and c to give the additional shape 'rectangle' as an option in MENU2. (You will need to make additions in MENU2 and OUTPUT and write an additional procedure DRAWRECT.)

SUMMARY

In this chapter we have met some of the various uses for colour and graphics in presenting attractive screen images. These techniques, once learnt, can improve the presentation of almost any program written, and therefore it is a good idea to adopt good presentational practices from the start.

The approach to programming presented through the use of procedures in the last example is the most significant feature of the chapter. It is via the use of similar techniques, which are presented more formally later, that we shall approach more complex programming problems.

4 Do it Once, and Do it Again!

INTRODUCTION

In this chapter, we shall describe looping constructions available in BASIC. By looping, we mean repeatedly performing the same sequence of BASIC instructions.

There are several types of loop available to the programmer, but they fall into two broad classes: the count-controlled loop, and the condition-controlled loop. The condition-controlled loop will be our main concern in this chapter, while the count-controlled loop will be central to the processing of lists in Chapter 5. Our discussion of loops in this chapter is motivated by a consideration of computer security.

COMPUTER SECURITY

For a number of years now, one major problem of having large quantities of information stored on computer has been the worry that the information might fall into the wrong hands. It has therefore been necessary to devise various methods for controlling access to certain computer systems, and many of these security devices involve the use of passwords.

Users of bank and building society ATMs (Automated Teller Machines) will be familiar with the use of a PIN code (Personal Identification Number) which is used as a password along with a plastic card for the conduct of accounts at the ATM. Users of networked and large computer installations may also be familiar with the use of passwords to gain access to the computer system.

In this example, we consider the construction of a password routine to restrict access to a computer program. We shall write a short segment of BASIC which requests a password and checks the password typed in against the correct one — in this case **'CHESTER'**. If the user types in the correct password, then the computer will respond 'Welcome to the program', whereas a wrong password merely results in the computer requesting that the password be entered again. (We consider later how to make our program more realistic.)

The repetitive nature of this requirement can be recognised, since the request for a password is to be *repeated* until the correct password is input. It is worth remembering that whenever we think about a program and the word . . . UNTIL goes through our minds, then we are probably going to need an UNTIL loop. This is certainly the case in our present example.

Having decided to use an UNTIL loop, there are two standard questions which we must always ask ourselves:

Q. What do we need to do repeatedly?

A. Request a password

This defines the instructions which form the **body** of the loop.

Q. When do we stop?

A. When the password given is 'Chester'.

This defines the **exit condition** for the loop.

Programs 4.1a and b give some suitable BASIC commands to form the body of the loop.

Program 4.1a (RM BASIC)

CLS
HOME
PRINT "Type in your password"
INPUT Pass$

Program 4.1b (IBM BASICA)

CLS
PRINT "Type in your password"
INPUT PASS$

RM BASIC includes a REPEAT . . . UNTIL construction which provides precisely the loop control which we need. This reflects the trend (in more up-to-date implementations of BASIC) to supply the widest possible selection of control structures which then enable programs to be written easily. Program 4.2a illustrates the use of REPEAT . . . UNTIL in this way.

Turbo Basic provides a DO . . . LOOP UNTIL construction which is illustrated in Program 4.2b. This is an extension to the normal IBM BASIC loop control facility which does not provide an UNTIL structure; the use of WHILE loops is discussed below, and Program 4.3 illustrates how one could be used in this situation.

DO IT ONCE, AND DO IT AGAIN! 57

In each of these situations, the instructions in the *body* of the loop are executed repeatedly until the condition prescribed in the UNTIL clause is satisfied; execution then continues with the next statement after the end of the loop.

Program 4.2a (RM BASIC)

```
REPEAT
CLS
HOME
PRINT "Type in your password"
INPUT Pass$
UNTIL Pass$ = "Chester"
```

Program 4.2b (Turbo Basic)

```
DO
CLS
PRINT "Type in your password"
INPUT Pass$
LOOP UNTIL Pass$ = "Chester"
```

WHILE LOOPS

Essentially there are two different types of condition-controlled loops: the UNTIL loop and the WHILE loop. In almost every practical situation, either could be used interchangeably, although it is usually more convenient to use one type rather than the other. As a result of the interchangeability of UNTIL and WHILE loops, BASIC implementations often do not offer both constructions, but instead provide one or other, and expect the programmer to use the one provided.

IBM BASICA provides a WHILE . . . WEND facility. In order to understand how to use it, we need to appreciate the difference between an UNTIL loop and a WHILE loop. In both UNTIL and WHILE constructions, we have a collection of instructions which form the *body* of the loop, surrounded by the instructions which control the loop. The essential difference between the two types of loop is that, in the UNTIL loop, the condition is checked *at the end* of the instructions, whereas in a WHILE loop, the condition is checked *at the start* of the list.

Program 4.3 illustrates the WHILE loop construction for the password program for IBM BASICA.

Program 4.3 (IBM BASICA)

```
WHILE Pass$ <> "Chester"
CLS
PRINT "Type in the password"
```

```
INPUT Pass$
WEND
```

If we contrast the program segment in Program 4.3 with Program 4.2b, the difference is that on *entering* the loop for the *first time* the value of Pass$ is checked with the WHILE loop, and therefore the value of Pass$ must have been preset (so that it may be compared with "Chester"). If Pass$ did in fact contain the value "Chester" on initial entry to the WHILE loop, then the loop would be completely missed out by the computer, since the instruction is to execute the loop only **while Pass$ does not contain the word "Chester"**.

The UNTIL loop, on the other hand, does not perform any value checking at the start of the loop, and therefore the first value of Pass$ checked against the word "Chester" is at the end of the first 'pass' through the body of the loop.

The discussion above explains why, in practice, the program outlined in Program 4.3 will need to include some additional **initialisation** instructions to set up an original value of Pass$ which is not "Chester" (see Program 4.4.)

Program 4.4 (IBM BASICA)
```
Pass$ = "rubbish"
WHILE Pass$ <> "Chester"
PRINT "Type in your password"
INPUT Pass$
WEND
```

Note: as in the previous chapter, here we have presented a sequence of BASIC statements without line numbers. In order to execute the program segment described, it needs to be incorporated into a program with line numbers. To illustrate this, Programs 4.5a, b and c give fully operational versions of the programs developed above, to provide a basis for our subsequent discussions.

Program 4.5a (RM BASIC)
```
10  REM Password 1
20  REPEAT
30  CLS
40  HOME
50  PRINT "Type in your password"
60  INPUT Pass$
70  UNTIL Pass$ = "Chester"
80  PRINT "Password accepted, welcome to the program."
```

Program 4.5b (Turbo Basic)
```
10  REM Password
20  DO
30  CLS
40  PRINT "Type in your password"
```

```
50  INPUT Pass$
60  LOOP UNTIL Pass$ = "Chester"
70  PRINT "Password accepted, welcome to the program.
```

Program 4.5c (IBM BASICA)
```
10  REM Password
20  Pass$ = "rubbish"
30  WHILE Pass$ <> "Chester"
40  CLS
50  PRINT "Type in your password"
60  INPUT Pass$
70  WEND
80  PRINT "Password accepted, welcome to the program."
```

PROBLEMS WITH THE PASSWORD PROGRAM

There are essentially three problems with the programs listed in Programs 4.5a, b and c:

i) the password 'Chester' must be typed in *exactly as it appears in the program*, in order for the program to recognise it. In other words, **CHESTER** and **chester** would not be recognised as being the same password as **Chester**;

ii) the user is allowed an unlimited number of attemps to guess the password. This is unrealistic: most password systems allow only a small number of tries before refusing the user admittance;

iii) the system is not particularly secure, since the password is explicitly listed within the program.

We shall be able to deal with problems (i) and (ii) in this chapter, but we shall need to develop more sophisticated methods before we can cope with (iii).

Case Sensitivity

Case sensitivity describes the problem that **CHESTER** and **chester** are not recognised as being the same password as **Chester**. This is a direct result of the way in which the computer stores characters without identifying lower case and upper case versions of the same letter as being in any way related. The simplest way to overcome the problem of case sensitivity in a situation such as the present one is to use the BASIC words **OR** and **AND** to identify the acceptable alternatives. Thus the relevant lines of Programs 4.5a, b and c become respectively:

UNTIL (Pass$ = "Chester") OR (Pass$ = "CHESTER") OR (Pass$ = "chester")

```
LOOP UNTIL (Pass$ = "Chester") OR (Pass$ = "CHESTER") OR (Pass$
       = "chester")
WHILE (Pass$ <> "Chester") AND (Pass$ <> "CHESTER") AND (Pass$
       <> "chester")
```

Notice, in each case, the use of brackets around each of the alternatives linked by the OR/AND expressions.

Exercise A

Edit Program 4.5 to take account of the change described here, and run it to confirm that it is no longer case sensitive.

CONTROLLING THE NUMBER OF FAILURES

Most password systems allow users only a limited number of attemps at giving the password before rejecting them, the idea being that if the password is not correctly typed in on, say, the third occasion, then the user is probably guessing. We can build this checking into the program already developed by adding a few simple statements. The loop which we shall construct here is a special sort of condition-controlled loop, because the condition is partly dependent upon the value of a counter. (In the next chapter, we shall meet other loops which are controlled by a counter which use an alternative construction — the FOR . . NEXT loop.)

In order to make the desired change, it is necessary to introduce a numerical variable which counts the number of attempts so far. This type of variable is known as a *counter*, and it will be convenient to give it the identifier COUNT. (Notice how the identifier 'COUNT' does not end in a dollar and therefore defines a numerical variable.)

There are three steps involved in setting up a counter control in an UNTIL/WHILE loop: *Initialisation, Incrementation,* and *Checking*.

— **Initialisation:** this is how we describe the process of setting up the COUNT variable at the beginning of the loop. If the value COUNT is to record the number of attempts at typing in the password, then it must be given the value zero before the first attempt. This could be performed with the statement:

$$COUNT = 0$$

— **Incrementation:** this is the name given to the process of adding *one* to the value of COUNT after each attempt at typing in the password. The BASIC statement which performs this process is simply

$$COUNT = COUNT + 1$$

but it is worth looking at this statement in more detail for a moment to avoid misunderstandings later.

- **Remark: assignment statements and mathematical equations**

    The statement COUNT = COUNT + 1 is an *assignment* statement. In other words, the right-hand side of the equals sign is evaluated, and the answer is put into the storage location defined by the identifier on the left-hand side (ie the variable labelled COUNT). There is therefore no problem in the statement used here, which instructs the computer to take the existing value of COUNT, add 1 to it and store the answer as a new value of the variable COUNT. Unfortunately, this is in conflict with the *mathematical* meaning of the same expression, which would be viewed as an equation with no solutions. To try to overcome this (slight) contradiction, some computer languages, RM BASIC among them, have adopted := instead of just = in assignment statements. Thus, the above BASIC statement would appear in program listings in RM BASIC as:

    COUNT := COUNT + 1

    This happens automatically, and there is no need for the user to insert the additional colon (:).

- **Checking:** this involves the addition to the looping control of the check for exit when the counter reaches a prescribed value. In our present example, this will involve the addition of the words

    OR (COUNT = 3) or AND (COUNT <> 3)

    as appropriate, within the UNTIL/WHILE instruction controlling the loop.

Exercise B

Take a copy of the program in its current form, and study it carefully. Identify the following components:

i) before the loop begins;

ii) the 'body' of the loop;

iii) after the program exits from the loop.

Try to insert the Initialisation, Incrementation and Checking instructions in the appropriate places. (Programs 4.6a, b and c in Appendix 3 give one possible form of the correct program, but run your own version to see how well it works.)

If you have run your program carefully and noted its behaviour over a number of examples, you will have discovered that it is not yet complete! At present, after a third unsuccessful attempt to give the correct password, the user is admitted to the program anyway, with the words 'Welcome to the program.' This is obviously undesirable, and prompts us to add the following statement:

IF (PASS$ = "CHESTER") OR (PASS$ = "Chester") OR

(PASS$ = "chester") THEN PRINT "Welcome to the program" ELSE PRINT "GO AWAY":NEW

in place of the PRINT "Welcome . . . " statement in the previous version. This has the effect of only welcoming the user who gives the correct password, and has a particularly nasty effect on anyone who gives a wrong password three times in a row! (If you cannot tell what will happen in this case, then try it and see, but save your work on disk first!)

Exercise C

What is the effect of changing the condition just described into:

IF COUNT < 3 THEN PRINT "Welcome to the program" ELSE PRINT "GO AWAY":NEW

which is a shorter instruction and at a first glance would seem to do the same job?

HIDING THE PASSWORD

As we have already remarked, the password in this example would easily be discovered by anybody able to list the program statements on the screen or printer. It is therefore undesirable from a security point of view to have the password stored within the program file. An alternative would be to store the password in a 'file' on disk, possibly in an 'encrypted' form which would make it more difficult to discover. We shall be in a position to make this change in a later chapter.

Readers of this work who are using Turbo Basic have the advantage that, with a compiler, quite good protection is provided with the original program, if the compiled version (the 'object' or 'executable' code) is stored separately from the original BASIC program, and the original BASIC program is not released to users.

Exercise D

A shop needs to know what the average total takings of the assistants is at the end of each day. Unfortunately, there will be a different number of assistants each day, because of illness, etc.

We therefore need a program which will take in a list of amounts, calculate the total sales and how many assistants there are in the list, and divide to calculate the average. You may assume that a suitable way to indicate that the list is at an end is to type in an entry of 0 for the takings of one assistant.

Thus, a typical day's entry list might be:

150.50

250.78

391.96

183.06

0

This should be recorded by the computer as corresponding to the takings of four assistants (ie ignore the 0 at the end) at an average of 976.30/4 = 244.075.

(**Hint:** you will need to have a loop structure identifying the value 0 as the exit indicator, and maintain two values: the count, and the total. Check your program by running it several times with different numbers, and confirm your answers manually.)

(If you have severe problems in completing this exercise, a solution is given in Appendix 3, Programs 4.7a, b and c.

SUMMARY

In this chapter we have discussed the condition-controlled looping constructions characterised by the WHILE and UNTIL statements. The count-controlled FOR loop is described in Chapter 5.

5 Come to a Party!

INTRODUCTION

In this chapter, we shall design and produce some birthday party invitations. This requires the production of printed output, and we shall discuss the alternative methods for doing this. Later in the chapter, we meet the concept of a list (or array) of names, and we see how a **count controlled** FOR . . . NEXT loop can be used to process a list of names and to produce personalised party invitations. The techniques introduced in this chapter lead on to some useful example programs as exercises: name and address label production and personalised standard letters.

DESIGNING THE INVITATIONS

Imagine that you are holding a birthday or Christmas party. You will need to send out invitations to your guests that are attractively presented. Can we produce them using a computer program?

We have already met a range of graphics techniques which would make it possible to produce a suitable screen display for the invitations, but is it possible to produce a similar effect on paper?

There are two principal techniques for putting images onto paper. The simplest to implement involves the use of a '**screen dump**' utility. This utility allows the computer user, on giving an appropriate command, to produce a copy of the screen on paper at any given moment. On an IBM computer, the command consists of pressing a particular combination of keys when the required display is shown, and this results in the screen image being copied to the printer. Naturally, a black and white printer will give a black and white rendering of a display, no matter how many colours are shown on the screen. It is therefore often necessary to adjust and simplify the screen display in order to produce a good copy on paper.

In RM BASIC, the screen dumping utility is an 'add-on' to the language, and is unavailable unless the additional utility has been purchased and installed. When installed the command:

DUMP 0,0;639,249

produces a copy of the entire screen in 80 column mode, and:

DUMP 0,0;319,249

produces a copy of the entire screen in 40 column mode. This instruction would need to be included in the program at the appropriate point. The two, essentially different, techniques for producing screen dumps are thus illustrated — one needing user intervention when the required display is shown, and the other requiring a program modification.

Screen dumps are notoriously slow, since the screen image is reproduced by printing a dot image, ie a single black dot at every point which is to appear black. Thus, only a dot matrix printer or a laser printer can produce a screen dump, and all but the fastest of such printers will take several minutes to produce each page. In addition, the screen dump utility has to match closely with the the printer in use, and therefore when a printer is replaced by another model, it is not necessarily going to be possible to produce screen dumps using the same utility.

The alternative to producing a copy of a screen display is to generate printed output which is directed to the printer. This has the disadvantage that usually (unless the programmer is willing to become involved in some very lengthy and tedious programming) only text can be sent to the printer. However, the text may be formatted tidily with a little thought from the programmer, and this is much faster that producing a 'bit image' of the screen as in the case of the screen dump.

Output directed to the printer is usually produced using a slightly modified version of the standard BASIC PRINT command. Thus, the command to produce the word 'Hello' on the currently selected printer from within RM BASIC is:

PRINT   2 "Hello"

where the   2 directs the output to channel number 2   — the printer. Correspondingly, IBM BASICA uses the command

LPRINT "Hello"

LPRINT is used in many implementations of BASIC and is a reference to the standard output device which used to be connected to large computer systems — the lineprinter.

Exercise A

As we have just discussed, the alternative ways to produce an invitation involve

COME TO A PARTY! 67

either the use of graphics followed by a screen dump, or the use of text only by means of modified PRINT commands. For this exercise design two invitations. Your first invitation should use graphical images, and your second should be confined to the use of PRINT statements to produce a design that is text only. Write short segments of BASIC to produce each of these invitation designs *on the screen.*

Notes

1. It is suggested that you produce 'mock-ups' of the party invitations on the screen rather than on paper. This is a sensible way to proceed, since it avoids wasting paper while the program is being developed.
2. In the program which uses only PRINT statements, you need to avoid using those statements which move the cursor around the screen, since these will not be accepted by the printer. Instead, if you want to miss a line, simply use a PRINT statement on its own, and should you want to write 'Come to My Party' in the middle of the screen, use the instruction:

    PRINT "   Come to My Party"

with the positioning determined by the number of spaces inside the inverted commas (").

MAKING A START ON THE MAIN PROGRAM

Having designed the appearance of the invitations, we are in a position to begin to think more clearly about the actual task of producing a set of personalised invitations. If we were organising a party in real life, then we would need to undertake three principal tasks:

a) decide on the venue, date and time of the party;

b) decide who is to be invited;

c) write out and dispatch the invitations.

In order to get our computer program to produce the invitations, we shall need to write a program which takes the same amount of information into account as would be needed if we were producing the invitations by hand. It will therefore make sense for us to consider the computer program in three main sections — each of the sections will be implemented by means of a procedure.

The three parts of the program will consist of:

A Find out about the party — procedure PARTYINFO.

B Find out about the guests — procedure GUESTINFO.

C Print the invitations — procedure INVITE.

Once these decisions have been made, we may write the main 'driving routine' part of the program, which emphasises the overall structure and the reliance on the three procedures defined here. Program 5.1a gives the RM BASIC version of the main program.

Program 5.1a

```
10  REM Party Invitation Program
20  GLOBAL
30  PARTYINFO
40  GUESTINFO
50  INVITE
60  END
```

Note the use of the statement GLOBAL at line 20. We shall need to complete the detail of this instruction later before the program will run, but we have incorporated it here in readiness for later use.

Program 5.1b gives the corresponding Turbo Basic version of the main driving program.

Program 5.1b

```
10  REM Party Invitation Program
20  CALL PARTYINFO
30  CALL GUESTINFO
40  CALL INVITE
50  END
```

Program 5.1c gives the IBM BASICA version of the corresponding section of the program:

Program 5.1c

```
10  REM Party Invitation
20  GOSUB 1000 : REM Partyinfo
30  GOSUB 2000 : REM Guestinfo
40  GOSUB 3000 : REM invite
50  END
```

We now turn our attention to consider the three separate procedures.

PROCEDURE PARTYINFO

In this procedure, we shall need to accept as input, details of the venue, time and date of the party, and the name of the sender of the invitations. Suitable BASIC statements to perform this function are listed in Program 5.2.

Program 5.2 The Procedure PARTYINFO

```
PRINT "Type in the name of the person whose party it is"
INPUT NAME$
```

COME TO A PARTY!

PRINT "Type in place where the party is to be held"
INPUT PLACE$
PRINT "Type in the date of the party"
INPUT D$
PRINT "Type in starting time for the party"
INPUT T$

Notice that we have not used variables TIME$ or DATE$ to hold the time and date of the party; this is to avoid possible conflict with the variables often built into the BASIC system, which hold the current time and date.

In order to incorporate the code as part of the program, we need to use the appropriate additional instructions as shown in Program 5.3.

Program 5.3a RM BASIC

PROCEDURE Partyinfo
GLOBAL Name$, Place$, T$, D$
(code listed above)
ENDPROC

Program 5.3b Turbo Basic

SUB Partyinfo
SHARED Name$, Place$, T$, D$
(code listed above)
END SUB

Program 5.3c IBM BASICA

1000   REM Partyinfo
1010
1020   (code listed above)
1030   etc
1999   RETURN

Remark on GLOBAL in RM BASIC and SHARED in Turbo Basic:

The purpose of the GLOBAL and SHARED statements is to list *all* the variables used within a procedure *which will also be needed outside of the procedure.* In this way the computer is informed that references to a variable by that name, *within* the procedure, refer to exactly the same variable as is referred to by the same name *outside* the procedure. When we have written more complicated programs which use a more sophisticated hierarchy of procedures, we shall discuss this again. For the present, it is clear that the GLOBAL/SHARED statements in procedure PARTYINFO need to contain the variable names which we have listed in Programs 5.3a, b and c.

The GLOBAL statement at the beginning of the program will need to contain all the variable names which occur in GLOBAL statements elsewhere. This explains the remark which was made earlier, that we were unable at that time to specify the contents of the GLOBAL statement, but we could predict that one would be needed. For technical reasons, no corresponding SHARED statement is needed at the beginning of a Turbo Basic program.

PROCEDURE GUESTINFO — A Simplified Version

As a first attempt at getting the program working, let us assume that we have a guestlist containing only one name! This simplifies the situation somewhat, and will provide us with a useful insight into how the procedures GUESTINFO and INVITE inter-relate. We shall then be able to modify them later to take account of a longer guestlist.

In this restricted situation, the instructions needed in procedure GUESTINFO are simple, and are listed in Program 5.4.

Program 5.4 The Procedure GUESTINFO (simplified)

```
PRINT "Type in guest's name"
INPUT GUEST$
```

As in Programs 5.3a, b and c these instructions can be incorporated into the program by adding the appropriate statement to identify it as a procedure. Correspondingly, we may now write a simple procedure INVITE to combine the data and produce the invitation.

PROCEDURE INVITE — A Simplified Version

An earlier exercise in this chapter invited the reader to produce *two* different invitations — one using PRINT statements only, and the other incorporating graphics. Ideally, the statements used there should be incorporated now to make the procedure INVITE. However, for completeness, and to provide assistance to those who have not yet completed the earlier exercise, Program 5.5 shows a very rudimentary set of instructions to produce an invitation.

Program 5.5 The Procedure INVITE (simplified)

```
CLS
HOME (RM BASIC only)
PRINT "Come to a party"; GUEST$
PRINT "on"; D$, T$
PRINT "at"; PLACE$
PRINT "Please come!"
PRINT "from"; NAME$
```

Once again, extra lines need to be added as in Program 5.3 before this can be incorporated as a procedure.

COME TO A PARTY!

Exercise B

All the necessary 'building blocks' (procedures) are now available to you to produce a single invitation on the computer screen. Write out the full program on paper and then try running it. (Programs 5.6a, b and c in Appendix 3 should rescue you if you are in difficulties.)

CHANGING THE INVITATION

One of the most important aspects of writing programs using procedures, is the way in which it helps to focus our attention on a particular part of the program if we need to make any changes.

The program which we are currently considering has three procedures: two separate data entry procedures and one output routine. If we wish to change the appearance of the output by redesigning the invitations, we need only therefore make changes to the procedure INVITE. Thus we may think of the procedure INVITE as a 'bolt-on' module which can be removed and replaced with an alternative module. The only requirements on the replacement module are that it needs to 'fit', in other words, since INVITE expects the name of the sender to be stored as NAME$, the time as T$, and so on, the new module must expect the same. In the same way, you may make changes to the data entry screens, and as long as the existing modules are replaced with new modules which *return the same data in the same form* to the main driving program, these changes may be made without difficulty.

This illustrates another powerful feature of the writing of programs using procedures. Many programs that are written cover broadly similar ground. Often a new program will be written wholly or in part by taking procedures which have already been developed for other programs, but which serve the correct purpose, linking them by means of a new 'driving' program. This is obviously very efficient use of programming time and effort, but at least equally significant is the assurance — brought by using tried and tested procedures — that the resulting program will be free from errors.

THE NEED FOR LISTS

The party invitation program which we have just developed suffers from the inability to cope happily with more than one guest. A very simple modification to the main driving program can be made which overcomes this problem (see Program 5.7a, b and c). However, this solution is not wholly satisfactory, because it would be better to first put in the whole list of guests and then for the computer to produce the entire set of invitations in one complete batch. (The Program 5.7 solutions have the computer printing out the invitations one at a time and then asking for the name of the next guest.)

Program 5.7a (RM BASIC)

```
10  REM Party Invitation Program
20  GLOBAL
30  PARTYINFO
33  PRINT "How many guests will there be?"
35  INPUT Number
37  FOR I = 1 TO Number
40  GUESTINFO
50  INVITE
55  NEXT I
60  END
```

Program 5.7b (Turbo Basic)

```
10  REM Party Invitation Program
20  CALL PARTYINFO
23  PRINT "How many guests will there be?"
25  INPUT Number
27  FOR I = 1 TO Number
30  CALL GUESTINFO
40  CALL INVITE
45  NEXT I
50  END
```

Program 5.7c (IBM BASICA)

```
10  REM Party Invitation
20  GOSUB 1000 : REM Partyinfo
23  PRINT "How many guests will there be?"
25  INPUT Number
27  FOR I = 1 TO Number
30  GOSUB 2000 : REM Guestinfo
40  GOSUB 3000 : REM Invite
45  NEXT I
50  END
```

A more correct approach for us to take, is to reflect in the computer program the standard processes which would be involved in the normal manual scheme: decide on the party details, make the guest list, make out the invitations. In order to achieve this, we shall need to store a **list** of names in the computer, and so we are prompted to ask the question: 'How is a list stored in the computer?'

ARRAYS

The storage of either lists or tables in BASIC is performed using a structure known as an *array*. An array may contain either only numerical entries, or only string entries. As with simple variables, strings are distinguished from numerical variables by the presence of the $ sign at the end of their identifiers.

In order to use an array, space must be reserved for it before it may be referenced. This is done using a DIM statement, where DIM gives the **dimension** of the array. Thus, for example, DIM FRED(45) would set up a list called FRED which could contain 45 entries; while DIM X$(76) would set up a variable called X$ which has space for 76 string variables. We shall discuss arrays of two (or more) dimensions in a later chapter, when we need to store data in tabular form.

By way of a concrete example, we could have an array called STUDENT$ which has been set up using the statement DIM STUDENT$(10). Then STUDENT$( ) is an array with space for 10 strings, which could be used to store the first names of 10 students. We may think of the DIM statement as reserving the empty structure shown in Figure 5.1a, in readiness for us to store the list of names there. Data is put into the array using the array **index** which indicates which numbered entry in the array is referenced. Thus the statement:

STUDENT$(1) = "Mike"

would result in the array contents being as indicated in Figure 5.1b and the statement:

STUDENT$(9) = "Sarah"

would result in the array being as in Figure 5.1c.

More useful in practice than this method for addressing individual entries in the array is the use of a **looping** construction which will reference each element in turn. The appropriate loop to use in this case is the FOR . . . NEXT loop, rather than the WHILE/UNTIL loop, because the input of the data is controlled by *the number of data items to be stored within the array,* rather than by *a certain condition being satisfied.* (It may sometimes be appropriate to use a condition-controlled loop with a counter to reference the elements of an array when the work is not controlled by a need to process a fixed number of data items.) A suitable FOR . . . NEXT construction for the present situation would be (see Program 5.8):

Program 5.8. A FOR . . . NEXT loop to input the entries to the list

FOR I = 1 TO 10
PRINT "Type in name of student";I
INPUT STUDENT$(I)
NEXT I

This loop would cause names to be stored in turn in the first, second, third, etc, entry of the list STUDENT$. Notice how the FOR . . . NEXT construction surrounds the body of the loop in the same ways as the REPEAT/UNTIL

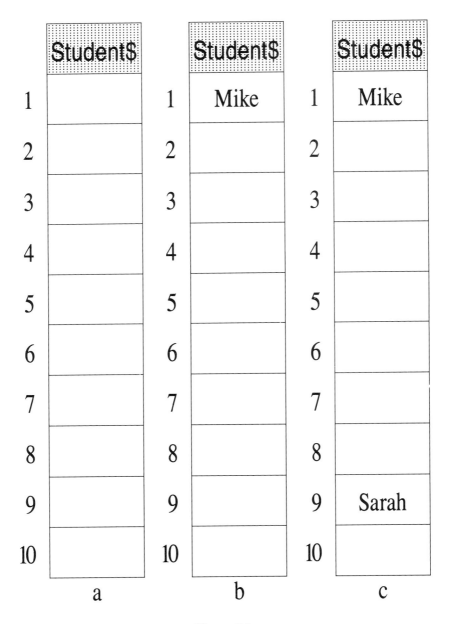

Figure 5.1

WHILE/WEND constructions did previously. These FOR . . . NEXT loops may be used in any situation where a particular set of commands are to be repeated a *fixed* number of times. Hence to write the word 'Hello' on the screen 100 times, we could use the instructions:

```
FOR I = 1 TO 100
PRINT "Hello"
NEXT I
```

The variable used to count how many times the loop has been executed (I in this example) is sometimes referred to as the 'control' variable of the loop. It is important to notice that in the first example (Program 5.8), the control variable does more than just control the loop. It is also *used* as an index to control which entry in the array is currently being accessed.

Two Types of Loop

We have now met both fundamental types of looping construction: the count-controlled loop, and the condition-controlled loop.

The crucial question in deciding whether to use a count-controlled (FOR/NEXT) loop or a condition-controlled (REPEAT/UNTIL or WHILE/WEND) loop is to ask 'When should the repetition stop?' If the answer is 'After . . . times' then this indicates a count-controlled loop, whereas if the answer is 'when . . . ' then it suggests a condition-controlled loop. But, in addition, we have already demonstrated (in the password program in an earlier chapter) how a counter may be incorporated in a condition-controlled loop. The general rule is: if there is any doubt, a condition-controlled loop is safer, although where it is the appropriate choice, the FOR/NEXT construction is the easier to use.

Incorporating the Array into the Program

If we refer back to Program 5.4 we see the procedure GUESTINFO which we used previously to record the information about a single guest in readiness for us to produce the party invitation. From an analogy with Program 5.8 we may use the segment of code in Program 5.9 to adapt the existing procedure GUESTINFO to use the array GUEST$( ) in place of the single variable GUEST$.

Program 5.9

```
PRINT "How many guests are there to be?"
INPUT GUESTNO
DIM GUEST$(GUESTNO)
FOR I = 1 to GUESTNO
PRINT "Type in guest number"; I
```

INPUT GUEST$(I)
NEXT I

Note that users of RM BASIC will need to incorporate a GLOBAL statement of the form:

GLOBAL GUESTNO, GUEST$( )

at the beginning of this procedure and add the variables GUESTNO, and GUEST$( ) to the GLOBAL statement at the beginning of the main program. A corresponding SHARED statement is needed by users of Turbo Basic at the beginning of the procedure only.

It is then a relatively simple matter to incorporate the additional looping construction into procedure INVITE, in order to print out a series of invitations on the computer screen, which correspond to the names stored in the array GUEST$( ). Once again, RM BASIC users will need to adapt the GLOBAL statement in procedure INVITE to include GUEST$( ) and GUESTNO.

In order to encourage readers to attempt to produce the completed program without further assistance, a final version of the program is given in Appendix 3 (Programs 5.10a, b and c).

When the program runs, you will notice that the invitations flash rapidly on the screen, and only the final one is displayed for any period of time. This is unimportant in practice, because we really need to print the invitations out. Go back to the procedure INVITE and add the necessary commands to redirect the output to the printer (we discussed how this is done earlier in the chapter). On running the program, a set of party invitations should now be produced on your printer.

We have now reached the stage where several useful exercises may be undertaken. In the first exercise, the party invitation program is adapted to produce standard letters, personalised for a list of addressees, and the second exercise involves the production of name and address labels. These exercises are described, and a possible method for their completion is discussed in detail in the remaining pages of this chapter.

Exercise C

Produce a program which accepts a list of names and produces a personalised letter for each of the names on the list. In order to do this, we will look again at the overall structure of the program which we have just completed. The program broke down naturally into three subsections, corresponding to the three processes which we would undertake when arranging a party: decide on the party details, decide on the guest list, and finally produce the invitations.

In this new example, we need to do two things: decide on the list of recipients, and print out a letter to each of them. Thus the new program falls naturally

into two procedures.
- (i) Referring back to the procedure GUESTINFO in Program 5.9 write (on paper) a procedure PERSONLIST which will accept the names of the people who are to receive the letters.
- (ii) Compose a letter on paper. When you have decided what to say, write out a procedure LETTER which will make the letter appear *on the screen,* correctly formatted. Do not bother at this stage to include the name of the person to whom the letter is to be sent, but instead just have a line of the form:

    PRINT "Dear"
- (iii) Now that the two fundamental building blocks for the procedure have been designed, write the main 'driving' program instructions: all you need to do is to call the procedures PERSONLIST and LETTER in turn, and then END. (Look back at the main part of the invitation program if you get stuck.)
- (iv) Integrate the names of the recipients of the letters by including the name of the array where they are stored in the PRINT "Dear" statement, like this:

    PRINT "Dear"; ARRAYNAME$(I)

    You will also need to include a FOR/NEXT loop construction and, in the case of RM BASIC, the appropriate GLOBAL statements.
- (v) When the program is working with screen output, make the necessary alterations to enable printed output to be produced.

In Appendix 3, a suitable program is listed as Programs 5.11a, b and c.

Exercise D

Write a program which allows a list of names and addresses to be stored, and name and address labels to be printed out.

In a real application, we would wish to be able to type in a list of names and addresses and store them for use on subsequent occasions for the production of name and address labels. In this exercise, we will be unable to store the lists for later use, but in a later chapter we will discuss an additional procedure which would make this possible. For the present, we will be content to store the data temporarily during the program run.

In this situation, again, we have a problem which splits up naturally into two phases. In the first, the data entry phase, we will need to input the list of names and addresses and then in the second, the output phase, we need to print out the name and address labels.

The initial problem which must be overcome is how the data is to be *stored*. For example the following name and address:

Fred Smith
12 High Street
Anytown
Somecounty

takes up 4 lines, whereas other names and addresses might take more lines, according to whether post codes, house names and so on are included. The first essential thing to do in designing the solution to the problem is to decide on a fixed format, say, of one line for the name and four lines for the address, and then put every entry into this format. You will probably have seen forms that are filled in by hand which 'insist' that an address should fit into a particular 'template', and these often reflect the way in which the address will be stored in a computer. It does not matter if some of the lines of the address are left blank, but we cannot include any more lines than will fit.

Having made this policy decision on the 'shape' of the standard address, the above example could be fitted in like this:

Name	Fred Smith
Address1	12 High Street
Address2	Anytown
Address3	Somecounty
Address4	

Notice how Address4 has been left blank to reflect the fact that the 'template' does not exactly match up with the current item of data. There is a 'trade-off' between having a structure which is always sufficiently large to take account of any possible item, and wasting a lot of space within the computer which will almost never be needed.

Having established a way of storing the names and addresses, we are in a position to begin to write the procedures. We shall use *five* arrays: ADD1$( ), ADD2$( ), ADD3$( ), ADD4$( ) and NAME$( ).

(i) Write procedure ENTERLIST which accepts the list of names and addresses.

(ii) Write procedure LABELMAKER which processes the list of names and addresses and produces address labels *on the screen*.

(iii) Write the main program segment which calls the procedures ENTERLIST and LABELMAKER.

(iv) Adapt procedure LABELMAKER so that the output is redirected to the printer. If you have some printed labels available to you, then try to make your output fit neatly on the labels. (Hint: should the output for the labels

COME TO A PARTY!

be too close together vertically, then try outputting some blank lines to the printer.) If you have labels which have more than one label across the paper, then you have a much more difficult task!

Note: no complete solution to this exercise is given. It is intended that the reader should use this problem to test how well the material has been understood so far.

A FINAL WORD ABOUT DATA SECURITY

In the previous chapter, we discussed data security, and developed a password protection program. This program may be incorporated into the party invitation program in the form of a bolt-on procedure PASSWORD. The complete program is shown as Programs 5.12a, b and c.

Program 5.12a RM BASIC version

```
 10   REM Party Invitation Program
 20   GLOBAL Name$, Place$, T$, D$, Guest$
 25   Password
 30   Partyinfo
 40   Guestinfo
 50   Invite
 60   END
 70   PROCEDURE Partyinfo
 80   GLOBAL Name$, Place$, T$, D$
 90   PRINT "Type in the name of the person whose party it is"
100   INPUT Name$
110   PRINT "Type in the place where party is to be held"
120   INPUT Place$
130   PRINT "Type in the date of the party"
140   INPUT D$
150   PRINT "Type in starting time for the party"
160   INPUT T$
170   ENDPROC
180   PROCEDURE Guestinfo
190   GLOBAL Guest$
200   PRINT "Type in guest's name"
210   INPUT Guest$
220   ENDPROC
230   PROCEDURE Invite
240   GLOBAL Name$, Place$, T$, D$, Guest$
250   CLS
260   HOME
270   PRINT "Come to a party "; Guest$
280   PRINT "on "; D$, T$
```

290 PRINT "at "; Place$
300 PRINT "Please come!"
310 PRINT "from "; Name$
320 ENDPROC
330 PROCEDURE Password
340 Count := 0
350 REPEAT
360 CLS
370 HOME
380 PRINT "Type in your password"
390 INPUT Pass$
400 Count := Count + 1
410 UNTIL (Pass$ = "Chester") OR (Pass$ = "CHESTER") OR (Pass$ = "chester") OR (Count = 3)
420 IF (Pass$ ="Chester") OR (Pass$ = "CHESTER") OR (Pass$ = "chester") THEN PRINT "Password accepted, welcome to the program. "ELSE NEW
430 ENDPROC

Program 5.12b Turbo Basic version

REM Party Invitation Program
CALL Password
CALL Partyinfo
CALL Guestinfo
CALL Invite
END
SUB Partyinfo
SHARED Name$, Place$, T$, D$
PRINT "Type in the name of the person whose party it is"
INPUT Name$
PRINT "Type in the place where party is to be held"
INPUT Place$
PRINT "Type in the date of the party"
INPUT D$
PRINT "Type in the starting time for the party"
INPUT T$
END SUB
SUB Guestinfo
SHARED Guest$
PRINT "Type in guest's name"
INPUT Guest$
END SUB
SUB Invite

```
SHARED Name$, Place$, T$, D$, Guest$
CLS
PRINT "Come to a party"; Guest$
PRINT "on "; D$, T$
PRINT "at "; Place$
PRINT "Please come!"
PRINT "from "; Name$
END SUB
SUB Password
Count = 0
DO
CLS
PRINT "Type in your password"
INPUT Pass$
Count = Count + 1
LOOP UNTIL (Pass$ = "Chester") OR (Pass$ = "CHESTER") OR
(Pass$ = "chester") OR (Count = 3)
IF (Pass$ = "Chester") OR (Pass$ = "CHESTER") OR (Pass$ =
"chester") THEN PRINT "Password accepted, welcome to the program."
ELSE NEW
END SUB
```

Program 5.12c IBM BASICA version

```
  10   REM Party Invitation
  15   GOSUB 4000 : REM Password
  20   GOSUB 1000 : REM Partyinfo
  30   GOSUB 2000 : REM Guestinfo
  40   GOSUB 3000 : REM Invite
  50   END
1000   REM Partyinfo
1010   PRINT "Type in the name of the person whose party it is"
1020   INPUT Name$
1030   PRINT "Type in the place where the party is to be held"
1040   INPUT Place$
1050   PRINT "Type in the date of the party"
1060   INPUT D$
1070   PRINT "Type in starting time for the party"
1080   INPUT T$
1999   RETURN
2000   REM Guestinfo
2010   PRINT "Type in guest's name"
2020   INPUT Guest$
2030   RETURN
```

```
3000  REM Invite
3010  CLS
3020  PRINT "Come to a party "; Guest$
3030  PRINT "on "; D$,T$
3040  PRINT "at "; Place$
3050  PRINT "Please come!"
3060  PRINT "from "; Name$
3070  RETURN
4000  REM Password
4010  Count = 0
4020  Pass$ = "rubbish"
4030  WHILE (Pass$ <> "Chester") AND (Pass$ <> "CHESTER")
      AND (Pass$ <> "chester") AND (Count <> 3)
4040  CLS
4050  PRINT "Type in your password"
4060  INPUT Pass$
4070  Count = Count + 1
4080  WEND
4090  IF (Pass$ = "Chester") OR (Pass$ = "CHESTER") OR
      (Pass$ = "chester") THEN PRINT "Password accepted,
      welcome to the program" ELSE NEW
4100  RETURN
```

This further illustrates the advantage of writing programs which use procedures, as the programmer may then import whole procedures from one program to another, without having to rewrite or retest that part of the program.

Exercise E

Using the above example for guidance, incorporate the PASSWORD procedure into the two exercises which have just been completed.

SUMMARY

In this chapter we have introduced two features of fundamental importance in the development of almost all computer programs: the ability to construct a loop controlled by a counter — and to distinguish those occasions when this is the appropriate type of loop, from those when a condition-controlled loop (as discussed in Chapter 4) would be better suited. In addition we have introduced the use of arrays to store lists of data items.

6 Lots and Lots of Boxes

INTRODUCTION

For several reasons, it is often appropriate to draw a diagram to represent a computer program. Various alternative forms of diagram have been developed over the years, and, until relatively recently, the one most commonly used was the flowchart (see Figure 6.1). However, more recent developments in the properties of programming languages, notably the implementation of procedures, and an increasing desire to write programs which both satisfy their specifications and are *well-structured*, have led to alternative methods of representation becoming more popular. The method which we shall use here is based on *Jackson's Structure Diagrams*, which were originally developed as a method of representing the structure of data to be stored in a computer as well as the procedures used in the program.

WHY DRAW DIAGRAMS?

The reasons for expressing programs in a diagrammatic form are two-fold: to assist in program design, and to provide an illustration, at some later date, of how the program fits together to allow for maintenance and debugging. Therefore it is clear that any diagrammatic representation of a program *must* give a *simpler* representation of the program than can be seen from the program listing. One of the important criticisms of flowcharts has been that they are often as complex for the reader as the examination of the actual program statements. Indeed, if we carefully examine the flowchart in Figure 6.1, we can see that it fails even to represent accurately the structure of the program that it was designed alongside. We must always be aware of this potential problem when we draw structure diagrams. It is important to examine carefully the diagram to ensure that it gives a representation which is not oversimplified, and yet is easy enough to understand.

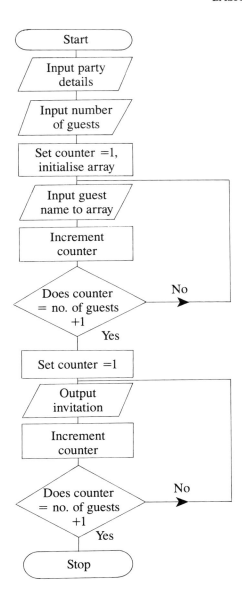

Figure 6.1 Flowchart Corresponding to the Program for Party Invitations From Chapter 5

AN EXAMPLE STRUCTURE DIAGRAM

Before we discuss the formal description of structure diagrams, we shall see how a structure diagram might be developed to represent the 'party invitation' program which was discussed in Chapter 5.

Note: structure diagrams are best used to represent programs which have been developed in a structured way. Indeed in later chapters we shall develop our programs using structure diagrams, and this will help to ensure that the programs are written in a structured way. Therefore, it is important to note, that using a structure diagram to represent a program which has already been written, is not always as straightforward as it is in the present case.

You will recall from the discussion in the previous chapter that we identified three distinct stages for arranging a party and dispatching the party invitations, which were written as separate procedures: PARTYINFO, GUESTINFO, and INVITE. This will form the basis for the first stage in drawing the structure diagram.

We begin by drawing a single rectangular box, and putting in the box the name of the problem which we are trying to solve, 'Party Invitations' (see Figure 6.2).

Having recognised that the solution to the problem subdivides neatly into three subsections, we draw *three* boxes on a level below the Party Invitations box, each joined to the box in the layer above, and each labelled appropriately (see Figure 6.3).

Notice how the procedures are represented in their logical order *across* the page *from left to right*, and the way in which they describe *in more detail* how the original task (given in the layer above) is to be performed.

Look at Figure 6.3, and consider the following question: 'Does the description in each of the three new boxes describe the process which that box represents in enough detail?' In other words, we need to decide whether, in each case, to leave the description in each at the current level of detail, or to introduce a further level of boxes *below the current one* which describes more fully what happens.

In order to make this clearer, first consider the procedure PARTYINFO. In this procedure, a number of questions are asked, and the responses are stored for later use. Thus the procedure could be described in the way shown in the structure diagram given in Figure 6.4.

Is Figure 6.4 clearer than Figure 6.3? Perhaps it is, in that it lists the precise pieces of data which are going to be collected. On the other hand, a program listing of procedure PARTYINFO would provide at least as much information and would be equally clear (see Figure 6.5). It is therefore inappropriate in this case to expand that particular box on the structure diagram in this way.

Figure 6.2 The First Stage in the Party Invitations Diagram

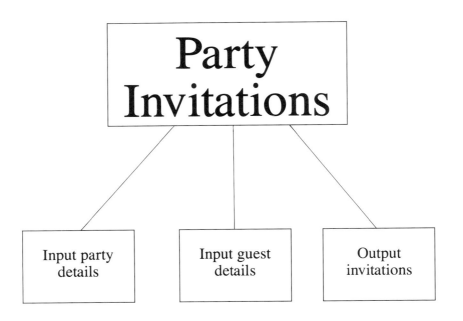

Figure 6.3 The Three Main Processes Are Identified

LOTS AND LOTS OF BOXES 87

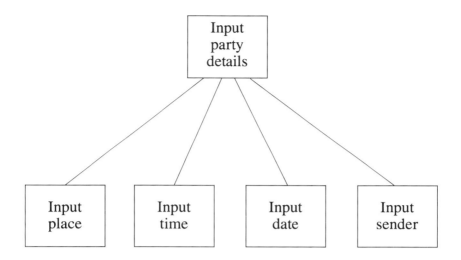

Figure 6.4 A Possible Simplification of the Input Party Details Procedure

When we consider the procedure GUESTINFO, however, we find a slightly different situation, because we are now trying to describe a looping construction in which the simple process of 'accept guest name' is repeated for each guest. Therefore we could expand the corresponding part of the structure diagram to reflect this (see Figure 6.6). In this case, the additional layer of the structure diagram does give more information than the previous version and is therefore justified. It is perhaps arguable that the procedure listing is still equally intelligible, but many people would feel in this case that the structure diagram was a *clearer* representation of the program.

```
PRINT "Type in the name of the person whose party it is"
INPUT NAME$
PRINT "Type in the place where the party is to be held"
INPUT PLACE$
PRINT "Type in the date of the party"
INPUT D$
PRINT "Type in starting time for the party"
INPUT T$
```

Figure 6.5   Procedure PARTYINFO

88 BASIC APPLICATIONS

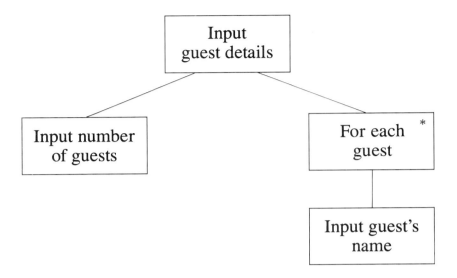

Figure 6.6 The 'Input Guest Details' Procedure May be Represented in Greater Detail, Which Emphasises the Loop Construction Used

It is useful to notice here the presence of the star (*) within the box on the structure diagram which refers to repetition. We shall discuss this more fully in the following sections.

Exercise

Sketch out a structure diagram which provides an additional level of detail for the procedure INVITE. (Appendix 3, Figure 6.7 provides a possible answer.)

SEQUENCE, SELECTION AND ITERATION

We are now in a better position to understand a slightly more formal approach to the definition and use of structure diagrams. Jackson's method of structured design is based upon the notion that all processes may be subdivided into three basic structures: *sequence, selection* and *iteration*.

— *sequence:* the simplest of the three fundamental structures is that which describes processes which are performed one after another. Thus, we are required to identify a *sequence* of operations (which may well correspond to procedures when we come to write our program), and we need to be

clear about the **order** in which they are performed;
- *selection:* it is not always possible to identify a set of processes which must be performed on every occasion; sometimes decisions must be taken which determine exactly which operations are appropriate in a particular instance;
- *iteration:* sometimes a particular process is to be repeated a number of times (as in the case of a program loop), and this repetition is termed **iteration**.

Jackson Structure Diagrams use a constant shape of 'box' to represent sequences, selections or iterations, but a star (*) is included in iteration boxes and a small circle (o) is included in selections (see Figure 6.8). We saw the iteration box used in Figure 6.6, while the selections were illustrated in Figure 3.14 in Chapter 3.

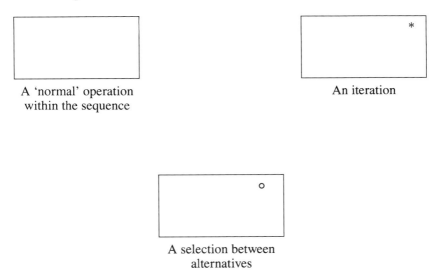

Figure 6.8 The Boxes used in Structure Diagrams

Take careful note of the general appearance of the structure diagrams. (This is particularly important if you are already familiar with the use of flowcharts, where the approach is completely different.) Here, the sequence of operation described in the structure diagram is illustrated by the *row* of boxes *across* the page. As we progress *down* the page, the boxes describe in *greater detail* how the tasks in the boxes on the layer above are to be undertaken. This serves to emphasise the programming methodology known as *'top-down design'* where the whole problem is expressed at the top level, and is gradually expressed in greater detail and simplified operations as we progress to lower levels of the diagram. This technique is also know as 'stepwise refinement' because of the action of *refining* (splitting up) each step into a number of smaller steps until each is a small enough task to program. (Yet another term used to describe this approach is 'divide and conquer'!)

PROGRAM DESIGN

We may use these structure diagrams as a tool in developing computer programs. In order to do this, begin with a *large* sheet of paper and draw a box in the centre at the top of the page. In this box goes a description of the whole task.

Next we need to consider how many sub-tasks the main task *naturally* splits into. These sub-tasks form the basis of the second row. (At this stage we do not need to know *how* each of these tasks is to be accomplished, it is sufficient to describe the tasks.)

We next take each of the sub-tasks and look at each *in isolation*. It is important to look at the tasks *separately* because this helps to avoid unnecessary complications brought in from other areas of the problem. It also helps when designing the program, to use procedures which concentrate on the task in hand and do not relate to other parts of the program in an unnatural way. In general, the procedures which we write are more likely to be usable for a similar task in other programs. Each sub-task is divided up by working successively down the page, until the description in each of the boxes at the bottom-most level is sufficiently clear and simple to allow a procedure to be written. It is then a straightforward task to write the program in terms of a sequence of procedures, each procedure corresponding to a box in the structure diagram.

Examples

Two examples are discussed below, and further example structure diagrams will be developed in later chapters.

Example 1

Books which deal with the design of programs almost always use at least one 'domestic' example to illustrate how the solution to a problem is subdivided into smaller procedures. Here we shall consider how toffee is made. The process of making toffee may be naturally divided into four sub-processes:

    a) collect all the necessary ingredients together;

    b) warm the ingredients in a pan and mix them up;

    c) boil until the toffee is ready (goes hard when a small amount of mixture

LOTS AND LOTS OF BOXES

is put into cold water);

d) pour out into a tray.

We may therefore begin our structure diagram as in Figure 6.9.

Considering the sub-processes in the second row of the diagram, it is apparent that neither of the first two are worth sub-dividing further, since the recipe list of ingredients would give a clearer statement of the items involved than would the structure diagram. We may however express the third box as an iteration as shown in Figure 6.10. Again, the fourth box is self-explanatory. The structure diagram in Figure 6.10 therefore gives a complete representation of the task.

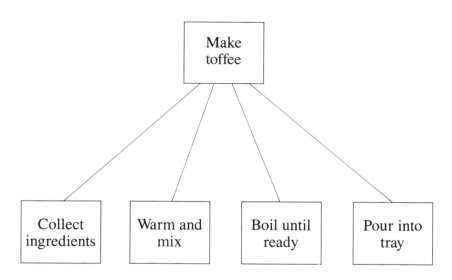

Figure 6.9   Toffee-making Structure Diagram, Stage 1

Example 2

In this second example, we discuss the construction of a structure diagram to represent a payroll system. This is necessarily a more complicated overall process, but it will become apparent that the structure diagram may be constructed quite simply.

To begin, we shall identify the processes involved in dealing with a single worker's pay, then we shall draw the structure diagram for the whole system.

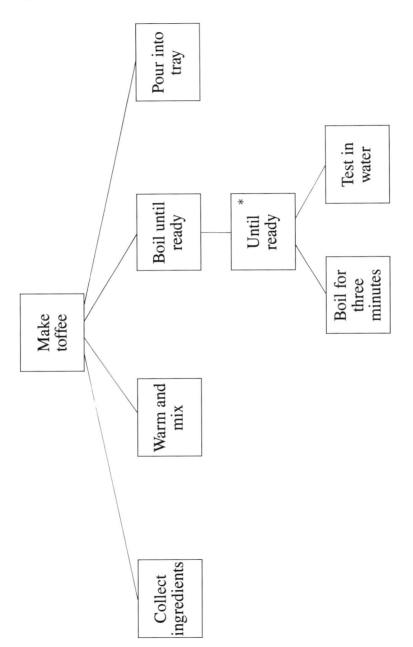

Figure 6.10 Completed Structure Diagram for Toffee-making

This approach is often a useful one to adopt, since by dealing with a simplified situation, we are able to come to a better understanding of the separate processes involved in the more complex case.

In order to calculate the pay of a *single* employee, we need to know some details *about the employee;* for example, what the hourly rate is, details of the tax code, etc. These are items of information which will remain (relatively) static and will only be updated occasionally. We also need to know about the relevant *current* information (for example, how much overtime has been worked this week, whether any absences owing to sickness will affect this week's pay, etc). We may assume that the *current* information will be collected each week, while the stored static information will be held separately. Therefore, the payroll calculations consist of identifying the two sets of information relating to the individual employee and then performing a standard calculation. Once the pay for the week has been calculated, the pay packet may be made up, and the payslip filled in. It is therefore appropriate to illustrate the payroll system *for a single employee* in a structure diagram, as in Figure 6.11.

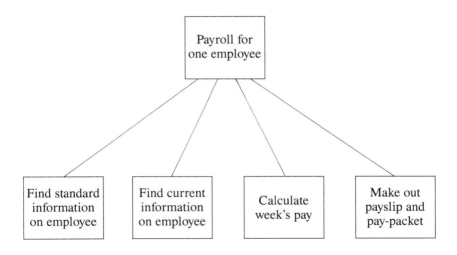

Figure 6.11 Simple One-Employee Payroll Calculation

We may now attempt to tackle the problem of designing a payroll process for a group of workers. Figure 6.12 gives a straightforward generalisation of the single worker situation described in Figure 6.11. However, for a number of reasons, the actual system likely to be employed in practice would not be the one represented in Figure 6.12. Figure 6.13 gives a more realistic description of a practical payroll system.

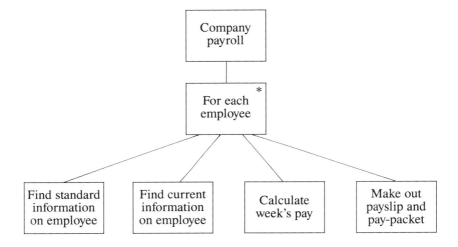

Figure 6.12   An Immediate Generalisation of 6.11 to Give a Payroll for Many Employees

Look at the two structure diagrams and see if you can see the advantages of the system shown in Figure 6.13 over Figure 6.12. The essential difference is that in Figure 6.13, all the tasks of each type are performed *together*. In other words, all the calculations are performed for all the workers and then all the pay packets are made up, whereas in Figure 6.12 each worker's pay is calculated and then the pay packet made up before the next worker's calculation is begun. The Figure 6.12 solution is therefore less likely to be satisfactory in a *manual* system because it does not provide for different people doing different parts of the job

In a *computerised* implementation of a payroll system too, the system outlined in Figure 6.13 is to be preferred, since it allows all the data to be entered in advance and then all the output to be generated together. As a general rule, better designed programs will cause all the output for a printer to be generated simultaneously. This means that, if necessary, the printer may be shared by several users without any single user monopolising it for a long period.

LOTS AND LOTS OF BOXES

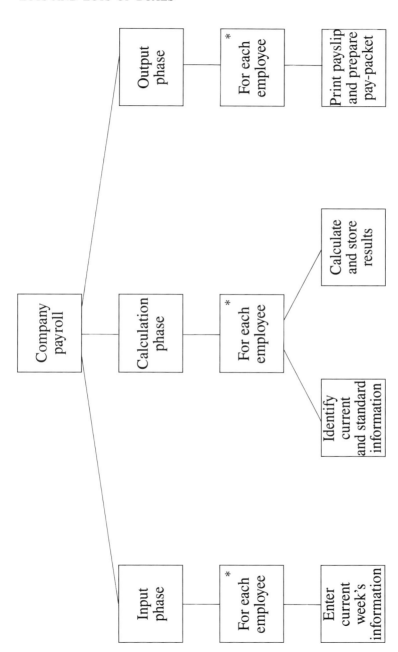

Figure 6.13 A More Realistic Payroll System

Exercise A

Many travel agents use computer terminals to provide an airline booking system, which gives details of seat availability and allows on-line booking of tickets. Try to draw a structure diagram which reflects how such a system might work. (Appendix 3, Figure 6.14 gives a possible solution.)

SUMMARY

In this chapter, we have met the idea of structure diagrams as a means of representing the inter-relationships between procedures which are to be used in a method for solving a particular problem. We shall use diagrams like these in the following chapters to assist us in designing programs that solve a series of realistic problems.

7 Hello, Can I Help You?

INTRODUCTION

In this chapter we shall begin to discuss a major programming project based around a mail-order company's computer system. Naturally we will study a slightly simplified situation to avoid becoming too involved in the fine detail of writing as sophisticated a program as this. Nevertheless, we will complete a realistic and working program in the following two chapters.

BACKGROUND

In order to begin any major programming project, we must start by reaching a clear understanding of exactly what our completed system needs to do. This aspect of the development of a computer program is usually undertaken, in large projects, by a team of **systems analysts.** They specify the requirements and design a possible solution, before briefing one or more programmers to turn the paper design into a real working program. However, it is increasingly common for programmers to assume this additional role, and to undertake the project right through from the initial investigation to the completed system. When one person undertakes this whole process, the term analyst/programmer is used.

Therefore, in our present example, we must begin with a clear statement of what will be required of our computer program. In a real situation we would begin by visiting the client and discussing the user's requirements and aspirations. We would then judge the current system, be it manual or computerised, against the requirements of the user. We could begin to design a replacement system, if appropriate, which would avoid at least some of the shortcomings of the existing system. Further details of this procedure will be found in any of the standard texts on systems analysis (see Appendix 2, Bibliography).

We shall restrict ourselves here to the 'tele-sales' operation of the mail order business in question. The requirements of the system are to allow the telephone operator to do the following using a computer keyboard:

1 Key in catalogue numbers of the required items.
2 Give details of the item's description, price and current stock level to the customer.
3 Take an order for the items.
4 Take details of the customer's name and address and payment method.
5 Output information for the dispatch department, an invoice for the customer, and management reports as necessary. (We shall discuss the appropriate types of management report later in this chapter.)

OUTLINE DESIGN OF THE SYSTEM

We have just outlined the requirements of our computerised system viewed from the tele-sales operators' standpoint. In this way, we may begin to map out an outline of an effective implementation of an appropriate system. Some initial thoughts on the overall pattern of the program may be presented in a diagram such as Figure 7.1.

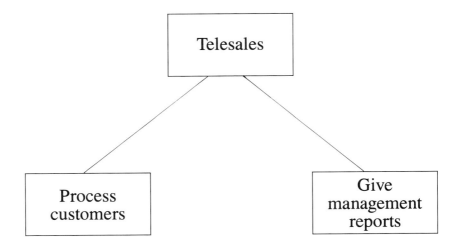

Figure 7.1 Initial Outline Plan for Telesales Program

In Figure 7.1 we have identified two substantially different phases in the operation of the required computer system. The processes numbered 1-4 given in the previous section have been identified as referring to the 'Process Customers' phase, while process 5 has been identified as separate, because it does not form part of the processing of individual customers.

Figure 7.1 is incomplete because no system can begin to process customers unprepared. There must always be an initial setting-up process before customers can be served. This is analogous to a manual system, where we might begin a day's activities by preparing a form with the date and the name of the telephone operator, in readiness for writing down orders. Indeed, as a general rule, we will find it necessary to have some sort of initial setting-up phase in almost all our programs before processing actually begins. Figure 7.2 takes this into account, and also represents a refinement of the customer processing part of Figure 7.1.

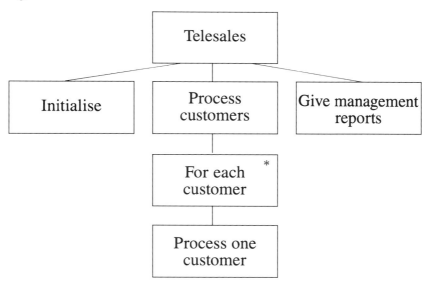

Figure 7.2 More Detailed Outline Plan for Telesales Program

Looking at Figure 7.2, we can see that only the customer processing part of the design is to be repeated. The initialisation process happens just once when things are started up. The customers are then processed repeatedly. Finally, after the last customer has been processed, the management summaries are produced.

We are now in a position to begin to consider the actual program.

THE MAIN DRIVING PROGRAM

We may, by analogy with the three principal processes in the structure diagram (Figure 7.2) structure the actual program in terms of three procedures:

1 procedure initialise;

2 procedure processcustomers;

3 procedure managementreports.

It is then a simple task to construct the main driving program (Programs 7.1a, b and c)

Program 7.1a (RM BASIC)

```
10  REM Mail order program 1
20  GLOBAL {to be completed later}
30  Initialise
40  Processcustomers
50  Managementreports
60  END
```

Program 7.1b (Turbo Basic)

```
10  REM Mail Order Program 1
20  Call Initialise
30  Call Processcustomers
40  Call Managementreports
50  END
```

Program 7.1c (IBM BASICA)

```
10  REM Mail Order Program
20  GOSUB 1000 : REM Initialise
30  GOSUB 2000 : REM Processcustomers
40  GOSUB 3000 : REM Managementreports
50  END
```

Before we can proceed to construct the necessary procedures, consideration should be given to exactly what data will be stored about the goods for sale; we also need to determine an appropriate storage method.

Catalogue Data Storage

A typical mail-order operation requires the availability of the following items of information about the items on offer:

1 catalogue number;

2 item description;

3 unit price;

4 current stock level.

In essence, therefore, we need to construct our program in such a way that a table of the following form can be stored (Figure 7.3).

Cat	Description	Price	Stock
123/4567	Teddy bear	£9.95	25
135/7912	Train set	£43.90	8
234/5678	Garden swing	£25.50	3

Figure 7.3 The Data to be Stored Will Have This Form

How should we store this information?

We have already met the idea of storing lists and tables using 'arrays', and this is an appropriate method of storage in this situation. However we do need to give careful consideration to the most appropriate way of using arrays in order to make the subsequent processing as easy as possible.

We may recall that within any list or table structure stored using an array, we need to insist that all the data items stored have the same fundamental type — ie we can either store everything as a number, or everything as a string, but we are not able to mix the two. Now, if we look at the data in Figure 7.3, we can see quite clearly that the descriptions must definitely be stored as strings. We are therefore prompted to consider the possibility of storing *all* the information as strings. Unfortunately, we cannot *calculate* using data stored as a string. It will be necessary to be able to calculate prices and new stock levels, thus it will be desirable to store these items as numerical data.

(**Note:** it is possible to use a rather complicated conversion technique to change values stored as string data into corresponding numerical values for calculation purposes, but we shall avoid this unnecessary complication for the moment.)

Figure 7.4 illustrates how four arrays may be used to store the data. All four arrays have the same number of entries and, for a particular stock item, the same index value applies across all four array columns.

As a final preparation for writing the initialisation procedure, we need to determine how large a range of goods we will have on offer (and therefore how big the arrays need to be). While we are developing a program we need to choose a manageably small size to avoid excessive typing, but a large enough size to allow for adequate testing. In this situation a size of ten would be appropriate.

Exercise A

Prepare a table in the style of Figure 7.4 giving details of the ten items which

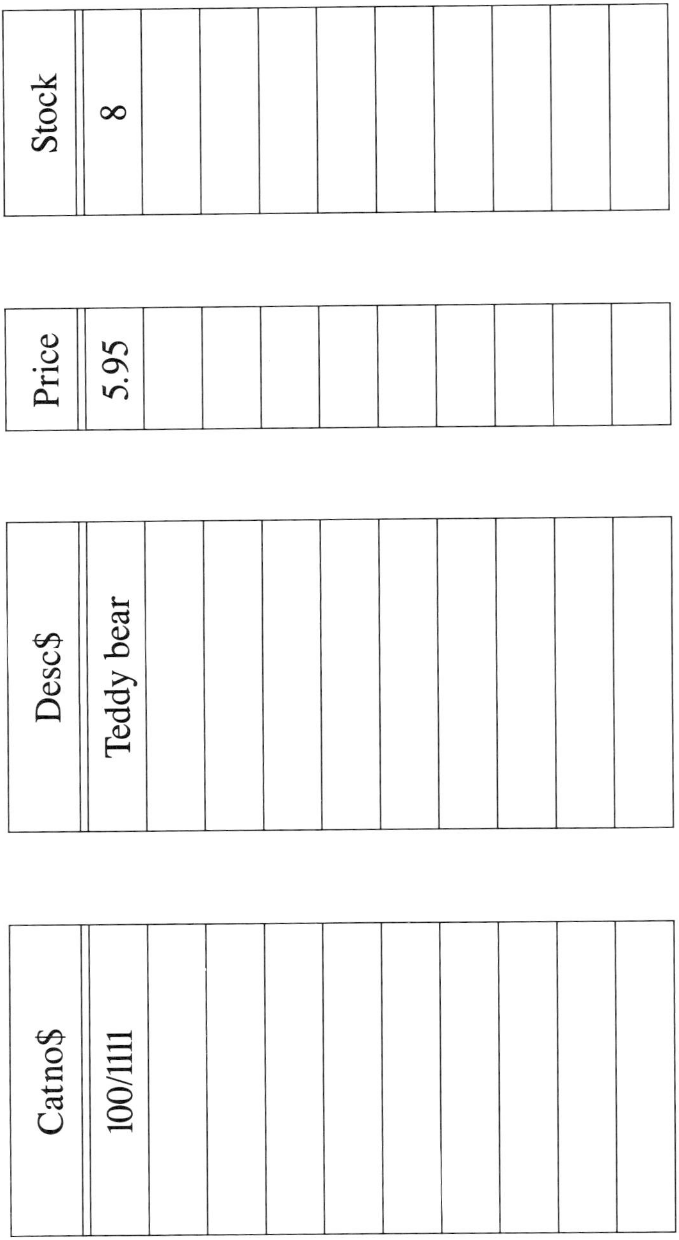

Catno$	Desc$	Price	Stock
100/1111	Teddy bear	5.95	8

Figure 7.4 The Data is to be Stored in Four Lists

the catalogue company will keep in stock.

THE INITIALISATION ROUTINE

We are now ready to begin writing the initialisation routine. This routine will consist of the computer reserving space for the arrays which we discussed, and reading the list of catalogue numbers, product descriptions, prices, and stock levels into the array ready to begin processing customers.

In order to transfer the lists of catalogue information into the arrays we shall use READ and DATA statements. READ and DATA allow for data items to be stored *within the computer program* rather than be input interactively from the keyboard, each time the program is run. With the increasing importance of interactive computer programs in recent years, the use of READ and DATA has become less significant. However, these statements do have their uses when we require 'static' data to be used every time the program is run, as in the present example.

Program 7.2 indicates how READ and DATA statements can be used in this situation. It is important to take careful note that there must be the correct number of data items and they must be of the *correct* type and in the correct order.

Notice how we have used a count-controlled FOR . . . NEXT loop to collect the data on the ten items of merchandise, and we have used a single DATA statement for each product. Within the DATA statement the separate items are surrounded by quote marks ("") whenever they are to be interpreted as string variables, and separated by commas in each case. Notice too how, because we have decided to store the prices as numerical rather than string values, we have been forced to remove the **£ symbol**. We shall, however, be able to reintroduce the £ in the screen and printer output in order to ensure that the prices are clearly represented.

Program 7.2

The use of READ and DATA to put the data into the necessary arrays

```
1000  REM Read in data to arrays
1010  DIM Desc$(10),Catno$(10),Price(10),Stock(10)
1020  FOR I=1 TO 10
1030  READ Catno$(I),Desc$(I),Price(I),Stock(I)
1040  NEXT I
1050  DATA "100/1111","Teddy bear",5.99,6
1060  DATA "101/2213","Radio",17.99,4
```

(Note: your program will need ten DATA lines which should include the ten items which you wish to sell.)

Exercise B

Try typing in Program 7.2 as a free-standing program and running it. Experiment with removing a comma or the quote marks ("") from some of the data items and familiarise yourself with the error reports which result. As usual, we must add the appropriate additional commands in order to make the instructions of Program 7.2 into a procedure within the current program (see Programs 7.3a, b and c).

Program 7.3a

Procedure Initialise (RM BASIC version)

```
1000    PROCEDURE Initialise
1005    GLOBAL Desc$( ),Catno$( ),Price( ),Stock( )
1010    DIM Desc$(10),Catno$(10),Price(10),Stock(10)
1020    FOR I=1 TO 10
1030    READ Catno$(I),Desc$(I),Price(I),Stock(I)
1040    NEXT I
1050    DATA "100/1111";"Teddy bear",5.99,6
1060    DATA "101/2213", "Radio",17.99,4
```

(Note: your program will need ten DATA lines which should include the ten items which you wish to sell.)

```
1150    ENDPROC
```

Program 7.3b

Procedure Initialise (Turbo Basic version)

```
1000    SUB Initialise
1005    SHARED Desc$( ),Catno$( ),Price( ),Stock( )
1010    DIM Desc$(10),Catno$(10),Price(10),Stock(10)
1020    FOR I=1 TO 10
1030    READ Catno$(I),Desc$(I),Price(I),Stock(I)
1040    NEXT I
1050    DATA "100/1111";"Teddy bear",5.99,6
1060    DATA "101/2213", "Radio",17.99,4
```

(Note: your program will need ten DATA lines which should include the ten items which you wish to sell.)

```
1150    END SUB
```

Program 7.3c

Procedure Initialise (IBM BASICA)

```
1000    REM Read in data to arrays
1010    DIM Desc$(10),Catno$(10),Price(10),Stock(10)
```

```
1020    FOR I=1 TO 10
1030    READ Catno$(I),Desc$(I),Price(I),Stock(I)
1040    NEXT I
1050    DATA "100/1111";"Teddy bear",5.99,6
1060    DATA "101/2213";"Radio",17.99,4
```
   (Note: your program will need ten DATA lines which should include the ten items which you wish to sell.)

```
1150    RETURN
```

Remark: the use of DATA statements to store the item descriptions, prices and catalogue numbers is appropriate since these will change only occasionally. Stock levels are subject to continuous change and so DATA statements are less appropriate here. In Chapter 8, we shall see how a more suitable alternative can be used.

PROCESSING A CUSTOMER

In order to simplify our initial attempt at the main customer-processing procedure, we will assume that each customer only wishes to purchase a single item from the catalogue. This avoids, for the time being, the problem of totalling up several different purchases. The method used to process a customer is summarised in Figure 7.5.

The processing of a single customer order can be subdivided into four main procedures:

Dataentry — where the catalogue number is recorded;

Information — where the computer searches for the details about the goods with the specified catalogue number and displays the information on the screen;

Purchase — where the customer decides to purchase, an invoice is prepared, and details are sent to the dispatch department;

Update — where stock totals and management information is recorded for subsequent use in the management summary procedure.

We shall consider each of these four procedures in turn:

Dataentry: procedure dataentry is basically simple and involves preparing a suitable screen display which invites the input of the catalogue number, and stores the value inputting as Cat$. Programming of this procedure is set below as an exercise.

Information: having accepted the catalogue number in the *Dataentry* procedure, we need to search the list of catalogue numbers until we find the one which matches the one entered. From a comparison with the problem of searching

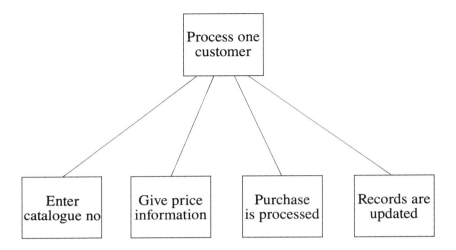

Figure 7.5 More Detailed Description of Single Customer Processing

a list by hand, we shall use an index which initially takes the value 1 (ie addresses the first entry in the list) and gradually works through the list one entry at a time, until either the correct entry is found, or the bottom of the list is reached. A **condition-controlled** loop is appropriate, because of the nature of this problem, and the overall looping construction very closely reflects the structure of the **Password program** in Chapter 4 (see Programs 7.4a, b and c)

Program 7.4a

Locating the correct item (RM BASIC version)

Counter=0
REPEAT
Counter=Counter+1
UNTIL (Catno$(Counter)=Cat$) OR (Counter=10)

Program 7.4b

Locating the correct item (Turbo Basic)

Counter=0

DO
Counter=Counter+1
UNTIL (Catno$(Counter)=Cat$) OR (Counter=10)

Program 7.4c

Locating the correct item (IBM BASICA)

Counter=1
WHILE (Catno$(Counter)<>Cat$) AND (Counter<10)
Counter=Counter+1
WEND

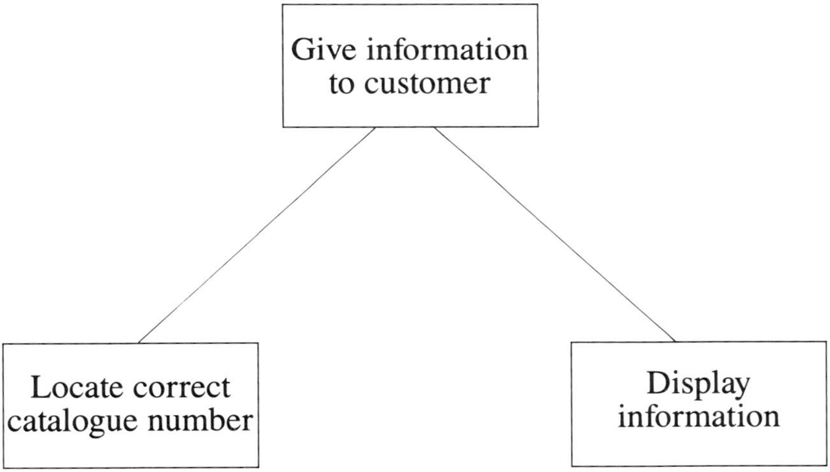

```
                  ┌─────────────────┐
                  │ Give information│
                  │   to customer   │
                  └─────────────────┘
                   /               \
   ┌──────────────────┐       ┌──────────────┐
   │ Locate correct   │       │   Display    │
   │ catalogue number │       │  information │
   └──────────────────┘       └──────────────┘
```

Figure 7.6 More Detailed Description of the Procedure Information

The purpose of Program 7.4 is to identify the index of the data item which we require. This is returned as the value of **Counter**. It is then a simple matter to print out the corresponding array entries to give description, price and stock levels. It is appropriate to summarise this in the structure diagram (Figure 7.6) and reflect this design by using the two procedures **Identify** and **Describe** as in the program segment given in Program 7.5. Notice the additional constraint which we have imposed in order to prevent Counter from being increased continually in the event that the data item we require is not in the list. Observe how this is used in the conditional call to procedure **Describe**.

Program 7.5

Procedures Information, Identify and Describe (RM BASIC)

```
PROCEDURE Information
GLOBAL Catno$( ),Desc$( ),Price( ),Stock( ),Counter,Cat$
Identify
IF Catno$(Counter)=Cat$ THEN Describe
ENDPROC

PROCEDURE Identify
GLOBAL Catno$( ),Cat$,Counter
Counter=0
REPEAT
Counter=Counter+1
UNTIL (Catno$(Counter)=Cat$) OR (Counter=10)
ENDPROC

PROCEDURE Describe
GLOBAL Catno$( ),Desc$( ),Price( ),Stock( ),Counter,Cat$
PRINT Catno$(Counter),Desc$(Counter)
PRINT "Stock";Stock(Counter)
PRINT "Price";Price(Counter)
ENDPROC
```

Exercise C

Rewrite Procedure Information in forms suitable for use with Turbo Basic and IBM BASICA. Note this simply involves the use of the alternative methods for calling procedures, and the use of the program segments given in Programs 7.4a, b and c.

Purchase: in this procedure, the customer decides whether to purchase the items, and the number required is identified. This is summarised in Figure 7.7, which identifies the separate procedures which we shall require.

a) Givequantity: this is a simple dataentry procedure which accepts the number required.

b) Decision: this procedure checks whether the purchase is to be permitted (ie checks the stock level against the number required), and calls a further procedure **Process** which actually processes the order, or the procedure **Error** which informs the user that the numbers required are not available.

A suitable example program segment to accomplish the requirements of procedure **Purchase** is given in Program 7.6, and examples of the printed output from the procedure are shown in Figure 7.8.

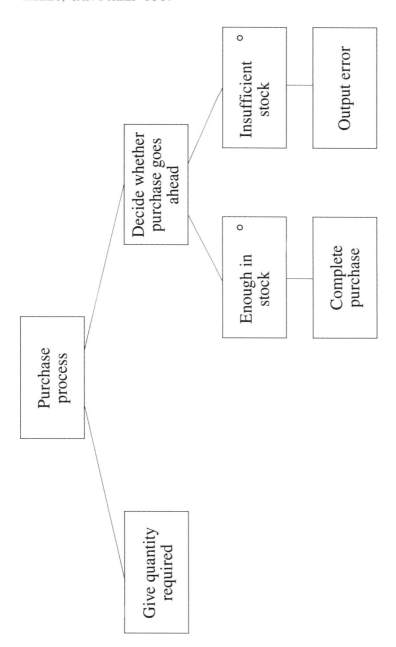

Figure 7.7 The Purchase Procedure Summarised

Program 7.6

Procedure Purchase (RM BASIC version)

```
PROCEDURE Purchase
GLOBAL Quantity,Counter,Desc$( ),Stock( ),Price( )
Givequantity
Decision
ENDPROC
PROCEDURE Givequantity
GLOBAL Quantity
PRINT "How many do you require?"
INPUT Quantity
ENDPROC
PROCEDURE Decision
GLOBAL Quantity,Counter,Desc$( ),Price( ),Stock( )
IF Quantity> Stock(Counter) THEN Error ELSE Process
ENDPROC
PROCEDURE Error
GLOBAL Quantity
PRINT "There is insufficient stock of that item"
Quantity=0
ENDPROC
PROCEDURE Process
GLOBAL Quantity,Counter,Price( ),Desc$( )
PRINT "Printing your receipt"
PRINT "Amount due =";Quantity*Price(Counter)
PRINT 2 "Receipt"
PRINT 2 "Purchase of ";Quantity;" of ";Desc$(Counter);" at ";Price(Counter)
PRINT 2 "Total Paid = ";Quantity*Price(Counter)
ENDPROC
```

Exercise D

Again, the translation of this program into versions suitable for Turbo Basic and IBM BASICA is very straightforward and is set below as an exercise. (Remember that LPRINT is the appropriate statement to redirect output to a printer in this case.)

Update: for the present, the procedure **Update** simply updates the stock levels in readiness for the next customer. Notice that the procedure **Error,** described above, reset the number of items required to zero so that *only the valid items actually purchased are subtracted from the stock levels.* It is within this procedure that we shall later include additional commands to provide more detailed management information.

> Purchase of 3 Teddy bear at 4.99
>
> Total paid = 14.97

Figure 7.8 Sample Receipt Output

This overall structure provides us with a collection of procedures for processing a single customer. This needs to be integrated within the main program to allow customers to be processed repeatedly within a single run of the program during a day. It is easiest to use some sort of condition-controlled loop which repeatedly calls the procedures for processing a single customer, but allows for a **rogue catalogue number**, say 999/9999 to cause the end of day reports to be produced, and the system to close down.

MANAGEMENT REPORTS

The final major part of the current program involves the production of management reports at the end of the day. We shall continue with our previous approach and subdivide this section into separate procedures:

Outofstock: which lists the catalogue numbers and descriptions of those items which have a stock level of zero.

Stocklist: which lists catalogue numbers and stock levels for *every* item, in order to allow for the data statements to be updated in readiness for the following day's transactions.

Turnover: which reports on the total value of sales for the day.

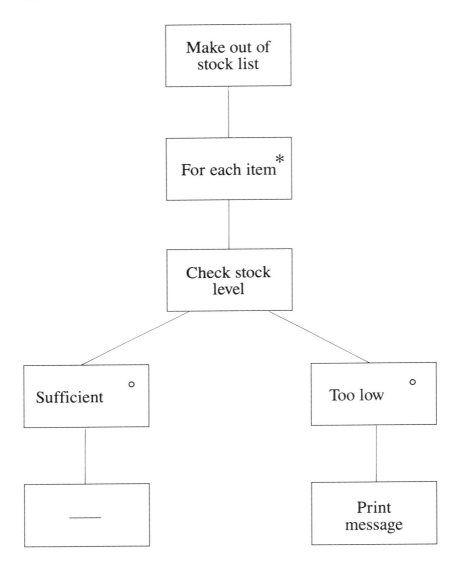

Figure 7.9 Out of Stock List Process

We shall briefly consider each of these procedures.

Outofstock: this procedure may be summarised in the structure diagram in Figure 7.9, which gives a simple statement of how a manual Out of Stock list would be prepared.

It is clear that the procedure consists of a loop which needs to be controlled by a counter, since we are able to predict in advance the actual *number* of items which need to be checked. It is also evident that a simple IF statement performs the necessary checks (see Program 7.7).

Program 7.7

Program segment to perform the Out of Stock list

FOR I=1 TO 10
IF Stock (I)=0 THEN PRINT Catno$(I), Desc$(I)
NEXT I

Stocklist: This procedure is very similar to **Outofstock**, but this time requires an output line for *every* catalogue item, and therefore no IF condition is necessary (see Program 7.8).

Program 7.8

Program segment to produce full Stock List on the screen

FOR I=1 TO 10
PRINT Catno$(I),Desc$(I),Stock(I)
NEXT I

Remark: Each of these procedures at present outputs the list to the screen. The usual simple changes to the print statements will redirect output to the printer if required.

Note: it might be apparent that the two procedures Outofstock and Stocklist could be combined in order to make a slightly more efficient program. The disadvantage of doing this is that it would result in the two reports' output to the printer being generated together, whereas it is more appropriate for the list of out of stock items to be separate from the overall stock list.

Turnover: the actual procedure **Turnover** is very simple because it only involves us in outputting the total sales value for the day. This may be achieved using a PRINT statement. Here it is more significant that we have not previously thought in explicit terms about the method needed to generate this total, although earlier we were able to identify the procedure **Update** as the appropriate place for the details about a sale to be recorded.

Suitable code for the procedure **Turnover** is listed in Program 7.9, and we can identify the use of the variable **Totsales** to store the total sales value for the day. We shall need to incorporate the statement:

Totsales=Totsales+Quantity*Price(Selection)

in the procedure **Information** and we shall also need to include the initialisation statement:

$$Totsales=0$$

in the procedure **Initialise.** Failure to include the latter statement would result in the value of Totsales being unassigned when the first customer is processed. Therefore the value after the first customer will be the **residual value** (whatever that might have been) plus the correct additional amount. The final day-total would therefore be in error by the same amount.

Program 7.9 Procedure Turnover

PROCEDURE Turnover
GLOBAL Totsales
PRINT "Total turnover for the day is";Totsales
ENDPROC

(The conversion of **Turnover** for alternative versions is set below as an exercise.)

The completed program, which is made up of all the procedures which we have been discussing in this chapter is listed as Programs 7.10 a,b and c. A pictoral representation of this program is given in the structure diagram in Figure 7.10.

Program 7.10a (RM BASIC)

```
  10   REM Mail order program 1
  20   GLOBAL Catno$(),Desc$(),Price(),Stock(),Counter,Cat$,
       Totsales,Quantity
  30   Initialise
  40   Processcustomers
  50   Managementreports
  60   END
1000   PROCEDURE Initialise
1005   GLOBAL Desc$(),Catno$(),Price(),Stock()
1010   DIM Desc$(10),Catno$(10),Price(10),Stock(10)
1020   FOR I=1 TO 10
1030   READ Catno$(I),Desc$(I),Price(I),Stock(I)
1040   NEXT I
1050   DATA "100/1111";"Teddy bear",5.99,6
1060   DATA "101/2213";"Radio",17.99,4
```
(Note: your program will need ten DATA lines which should include the ten items which you wish to sell.)

```
1200   ENDPROC
2000   PROCEDURE Processcustomers
```

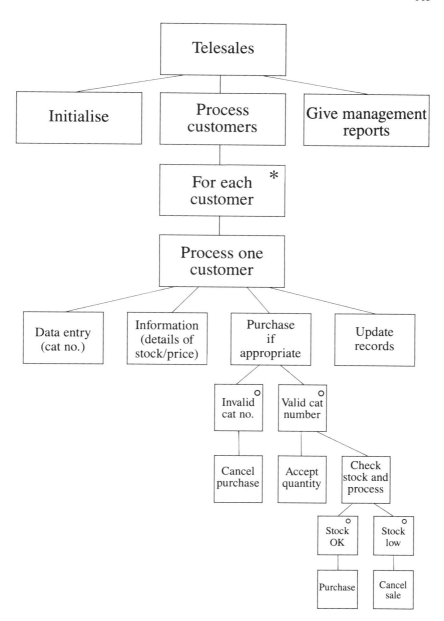

Figure 7.10 Complete Design for the Program Developed in Chapter 7

```
2010  GLOBAL Catno$(),Desc$(),Price(),Stock(),Counter,Cat$,
      Totsales, Quantity
2020  REPEAT
2030  Dataentry
2040  Information
2050  IF Catno$(Counter)=Cat$ THEN Purchase
2060  Update
2070  UNTIL Cat$="999/9999"
2080  ENDPROC
2100  PROCEDURE Dataentry
2110  GLOBAL Cat$
2120  PRINT "Enter catalogue number"
2130  INPUT Cat$
2140  ENDPROC
2150  PROCEDURE Information
2160  GLOBAL Catno$(),Desc$(),Price(),Stock(),Counter,Cat$
2170  Identify
2180  IF Catno$(Counter)=Cat$ THEN Describe
2190  ENDPROC
2200  PROCEDURE Identify
2210  GLOBAL Catno$(),Cat$,Counter
2220  Counter=1
2230  REPEAT
2240  Counter=Counter+1
2250  UNTIL (Catno$(Counter)=Cat$) OR (Counter=10)
2260  ENDPROC
2300  PROCEDURE Describe
2310  GLOBAL Catno$(),Desc$(),Price(),Stock(),Counter,Cat$
2320  PRINT Catno$(Counter),Desc$(Counter)
2330  PRINT "Stock";Stock(Counter)
2340  PRINT "Price";Price(Counter)
2350  ENDPROC
2400  PROCEDURE Purchase
2410  GLOBAL Quantity,Counter,Desc$(),Stock(),Price()
2420  Givequantity
2430  Decision
2440  ENDPROC
2500  PROCEDURE Givequantity
2510  GLOBAL Quantity
2520  PRINT "How many do you require?"
2530  INPUT Quantity
2540  ENDPROC
2600  PROCEDURE Decision
2610  GLOBAL Quantity,Counter,Desc$(),Price(),Stock()
```

```
2620  IF Quantity> Stock(Counter) THEN Error ELSE Process
2630  ENDPROC
2700  PROCEDURE Error
2710  GLOBAL Quantity
2720  PRINT "There is insufficient stock of that item"
2730  Quantity=0
2740  ENDPROC
2800  PROCEDURE Process
2810  GLOBAL Quantity,Counter,Price( ),Desc$( )
2820  PRINT "Printing your receipt"
2830  PRINT "Amount due = ";Quantity*Price(Counter)
2840  PRINT#2 "Receipt"
2850  PRINT#2 "Purchase of ";Quantity;"of";
      Desc$(Counter);"at";Price(Counter)
2860  PRINT#2 "Total Paid = "; Quantity*Price(Counter)
2870  ENDPROC
2900  PROCEDURE Update
2910  GLOBAL Quantity,Counter,Totsales,Stock( ),Price( )
2920  Stock(Counter)=Stock(Counter)−Quantity
2930  Totsales=Totsales+Price(Counter)*Quantity
2940  ENDPROC
3000  PROCEDURE Managementreports
3010  GLOBAL Stock( ),Catno$( ),Desc$( ),Totsales
3020  Outofstock
3030  Stocklist
3040  Turnover
3050  ENDPROC
3100  PROCEDURE Outofstock
3110  GLOBAL Stock( ),Catno$( ),Desc$( )
3120  FOR I=1 TO 10
3130  IF Stock (I)=0 THEN PRINT Catno$(I),Desc$(I)
3140  NEXT I
3150  ENDPROC
3200  PROCEDURE Stocklist
3210  GLOBAL Stock( ),Catno$( ),Desc$( )
3220  FOR I=1 TO 10
3230  PRINT Catno$(I),Desc$(I),Stock(I)
3240  NEXT I
3250  ENDPROC
3300  PROCEDURE Turnover
3310  GLOBAL Totsales
3320  PRINT "Total turnover for the day is ";Totsales
3330  ENDPROC
```

Program 7.10b Turbo Basic

```
10    REM Mail Order Program 1
20    Call Initialise
30    Call Processcustomers
40    Call Managementreports
50    END
1000  SUB Initialise
1005  SHARED Desc$( ),Catno$( ),Price( ),Stock( )
1010  DIM Desc$(10),Catno$(10),Price(10),Stock(10)
1020  FOR I=1 TO 10
1030  READ Catno$(I),Desc$(I),Price(I),Stock(I)
1040  NEXT I
1050  DATA "100/1111";"Teddy bear",5.99,6
1060  DATA "101/2213";"Radio", 17.99,4
```

(Note: Your program will need ten DATA lines which should include the ten items which you wish to sell.)

```
1200  END SUB
2000  SUB Processcustomers
2005  SHARED Desc$( ),Catno$( ),Price( ),Stock( ),Counter,Cat$,
      Totsales,Quantity
2020  DO
2030  CALL Dataentry
2040  CALL Information
2050  IF Catno$(Counter)=Cat$ THEN CALL Purchase
2060  CALL Update
2070  LOOP UNTIL Cat$="999/9999"
2080  END SUB
2100  SUB Dataentry
2110  SHARED Cat$
2120  PRINT "Enter catalogue number"
2130  INPUT Cat$
2140  END SUB
2150  SUB Information
2160  SHARED Catno$( ),Cat$( ),Desc$( ),Price( ),Stock( ),Counter
2170  CALL Identify
2180  IF Catno$(Counter)=Cat$ THEN CALL Describe
2190  END SUB
2200  SUB Identify
2210  SHARED Counter,Catno$( ),Cat$
2220  Counter=0
2230  DO
2240  Counter=Counter+1
```

```
2250    LOOP UNTIL (Catno$(Counter)=Cat$) OR (Counter=10)
2260    END SUB
2300    SUB Describe
2310    SHARED Catno$( ),Desc$( ),Price( ),Stock( ),Counter
2320    PRINT Catno$(Counter),Desc$(Counter)
2330    PRINT "Stock ";Stock(Counter)
2340    PRINT "Price "; Price(Counter)
2350    END SUB
2400    SUB Purchase
2410    SHARED Quantity,Counter,Desc$( ),Price( ),Stock( )
2420    CALL Givequantity
2430    CALL Decision
2440    END SUB
2500    SUB Givequantity
2510    SHARED Quantity
2520    PRINT "How many do you require?"
2530    INPUT Quantity
2540    END SUB
2600    SUB Decision
2610    SHARED Quantity,Counter,Desc$( ),Price( ),Stock( )
2620    IF Quantity>Stock(Counter) THEN CALL Errors ELSE
        CALL Process
2630    END SUB
2700    SUB Errors
2710    SHARED Quantity
2720    PRINT "There is insufficient stock of that item"
2730    Quantity=0
2740    END SUB
2800    SUB Process
2810    SHARED Desc$( ),Price( ),Quantity,Counter
2820    PRINT "Printing your receipt"
2830    PRINT "Amount due = ";Quantity*Price(Counter)
2840    LPRINT "Receipt"
2850    LPRINT "Purchase of ";Quantity; " of "; Desc$(Counter);"
        at "; Price (Counter)
2860    LPRINT "Total Paid = ";Quantity*Price(Counter)
2870    END SUB
2900    SUB Update
2910    SHARED Counter,Quantity,Totsales,Stock( ),Price( )
2920    Stock(Counter)=Stock(Counter)-Quantity
2930    Totsales=Totsales+Price(Counter)*Quantity
2940    END SUB
3000    SUB Managementreports
```

```
3010   SHARED Catno$( ),Desc$( ),Price( ),Stock( ),Totsales
3020   CALL Outofstock
3030   CALL Stocklist
3040   CALL Turnover
3050   END SUB
3100   SUB Outofstock
3110   SHARED Catno$( ),Desc$( )
3120   FOR I=1 TO 10
3130   IF Stock(I)=0 THEN PRINT Catno$(I),Desc$(I)
3140   NEXT I
3150   END SUB
3200   SUB Stocklist
3210   SHARED Catno$( ), Desc$( ), Stock( )
3220   FOR I=1 TO 10
3230   PRINT Catno$(I),Desc$(I),Stock(I)
3240   NEXT I
3250   END SUB
3300   SUB Turnover
3310   SHARED Totsales
3320   PRINT "Total turnover for the day is";Totsales
3330   END SUB
```

Program 7.10c (IBM BASICA)

```
  10   REM Mail Order Program
  20   GOSUB 1000 : REM Initialise
  30   GOSUB 2000 : REM Processcustomers
  40   GOSUB 3000 : REM Managementreports
  50   END
1000   REM Read in data to arrays
1010   DIM Desc$(10),Catno$(10),Price(10),Stock(10)
1020   FOR I=1 TO 10
1030   READ Catno$(I),Desc$(I),Price(I),Stock(I)
1040   NEXT I
1050   DATA "100/1111","Teddy bear",5.99,6
1060   DATA "101/2213","Radio", 17.99,4
```

(Note: Your program will need ten DATA lines which should include the ten items which you wish to sell.)

```
1200   RETURN
2000   REM Processcustomers
2010   Cat$="Begin"
2020   WHILE Cat$<> "999/9999"
2030   GOSUB 2100: REM Dataentry
2040   GOSUB 2150: REM Information
```

```
2050  IF Catno$(Counter)=Cat$ THEN GOSUB 2400:REM Purchase
2060  GOSUB 2900: REM Update
2070  WEND
2080  RETURN
2100  REM Dataentry
2110  PRINT "Enter catalogue number"
2120  INPUT Cat$
2130  RETURN
2150  REM Information
2160  GOSUB 2200 : REM Identify
2170  IF Catno$(Counter)=Cat$ THEN GOSUB 2300:REM Describe
2180  RETURN
2200  REM Identify
2210  Counter=1
2220  WHILE (Catno$(Counter)<>Cat$) AND (Counter<10)
2230  Counter=Counter+1
2240  WEND
2250  RETURN
2300  REM Describe
2310  PRINT Catno$(Counter)Desc$(Counter)
2320  PRINT "Stock "; Stock(Counter)
2330  PRINT "Price "; Price(Counter)
2340  RETURN
2400  REM Purchase
2410  GOSUB 2500: REM Givequantity
2420  GOSUB 2600: REM Decision
2430  RETURN
2500  REM Givequantity
2510  PRINT "How many do you require?"
2520  INPUT Quantity
2530  RETURN
2600  REM Decision
2610  IF Quantity>Stock(Counter) THEN GOSUB 2700 ELSE GOSUB 2800
2620  RETURN
2700  REM Errors
2710  PRINT "There is insufficient stock of that item"
2720  Quantity=0
2730  RETURN
2800  REM Process
2810  PRINT "Printing your receipt"
```

```
2820  PRINT "Amount due = ";Quantity*Price(Counter)
2830  LPRINT "Receipt"
2840  LPRINT "Purchase of ";Quantity;" of ";Desc$(Counter);
      " at ",Price(Counter)
2850  LPRINT "Total Paid = "; Quantity*Price(Counter)
2860  RETURN
2900  REM Update
2910  Stock(Counter)=Stock(Counter)−Quantity
2920  Totsales=Totsales+Price(Counter)*Quantity
2930  RETURN
3000  REM Managementreports
3010  GOSUB 3100 : REM Outofstock
3020  GOSUB 3200 : REM Stocklist
3030  GOSUB 3300 : REM Turnover
3040  RETURN
3100  REM Outofstock
3110  FOR I=1 TO 10
3120  IF Stock (I)=0 THEN PRINT Catno$(I),Desc$(I)
3130  NEXT I
3140  RETURN
3200  REM Stocklist
3210  FOR I=1 TO 10
3220  PRINT Catno$(I),Desc$(I),Stock(I)
3230  NEXT I
3240  RETURN
3300  REM Turnover
3310  PRINT "Total turnover for the day is ";Totsales
3320  RETURN
```

Exercise E

Type in and run the program. Examine the management reports and the appearance of the receipts and begin to make a list of some of the shortcomings which the program has. Make the list under the following headings:

(a) problems which make the program very unsatisfactory;

(b) problems which are inconvenient but could be accepted;

(c) problems related to the appearance of output.

The comments which you have listed under (c) are left for you to experiment to solve. Several of the issues which you may have listed under (a) and (b) will be considered in Chapter 8, but nevertheless, attempt to solve them for yourself now!

Look at the other two versions of the program. It is important to realise that although each of the three programs has been written to suit a particular *dialect* of BASIC, the fundamental design of the program is consistent in all three versions. You should be able to convert easily between the three versions of the program if you should ever need to.

SUMMARY

In this chapter we have tackled a large programming problem and come up with a design for a solution which can be implemented. We are able to identify several shortcomings to our solution, but it is important to realise that we have come fairly close to a usable program, and the discussion in the next chapter will result in a realistic simulation of a real-life package.

8 Can I Help You Again?

INTRODUCTION

In Chapter 7 we discussed a computer program which allowed us to operate a very simple simulation of a mail-order company's computerised tele-sales desk. You were left to consider the shortcomings of the limited system that was described. In this chapter we shall address some of these problems:

— some customers wish to buy several items;
— it is inconvenient to have to amend DATA statements to give stock levels each day;
— it would be useful to record the day-by-day summaries for month-end analysis.

SOME CUSTOMERS WISH TO BUY SEVERAL ITEMS

In Chapter 7, our program could only deal satisfactorily with customers who quoted a single catalogue number. It was possible for several identical items to be purchased, but if more than one catalogue number was needed, then the customer had to be treated as several separate customers. This is not quite sufficient, since it would imply the need to issue multiple receipts and invoices even though only one real transaction is involved. We shall therefore consider an amended design of the system which can take account of this.

Figures 8.1a, b and c indicate three alternative solutions, any of which would allow multiple items to be specified. In Figure 8.1a, each item is processed separately, but the information is stored until the order is complete, so that a single invoice/receipt is produced. The solution shown in Figure 8.1b has all the items entered in a list at the beginning and then all items are processed together. Figure 8.1c represents an alternative somewhere between the two others. Here the description of each of the items is found, and stock levels are checked, one-by-one during the initial input phase, but the items on the order are all stored and processed together.

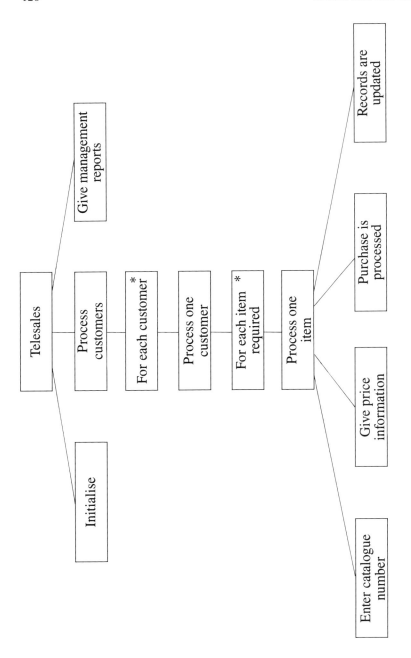

Figure 8.1a

CAN I HELP YOU AGAIN?

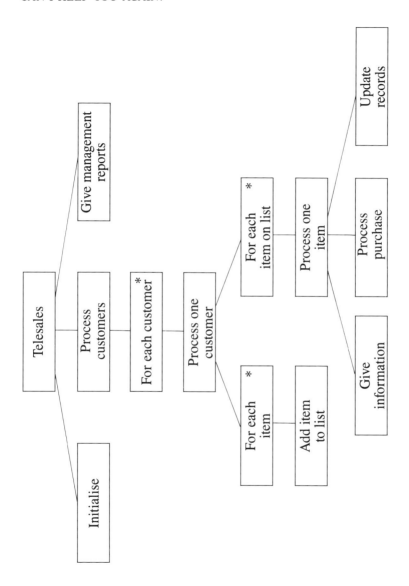

Figure 8.1b

128   BASIC APPLICATIONS

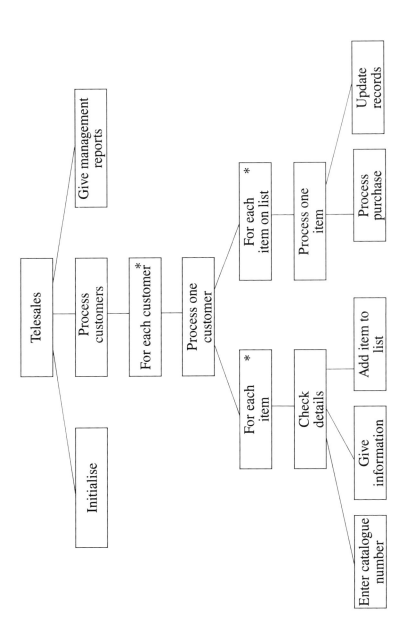

Figure 8.1c

CAN I HELP YOU AGAIN?

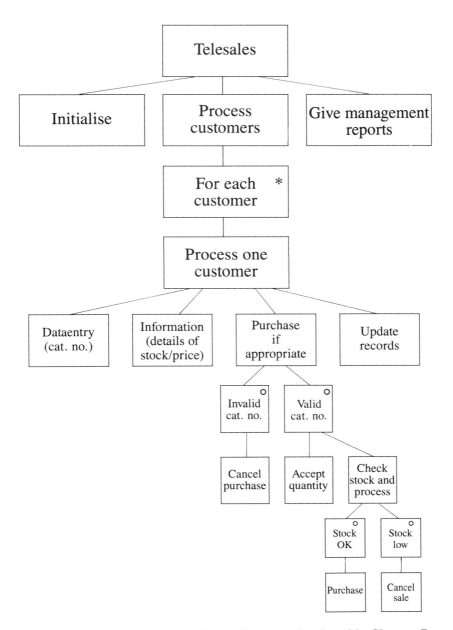

Figure 8.2 Complete Design for the Program Developed in Chapter 7

Of these three, Figure 8.1a is the solution which is closest to the one which we have already implemented in Chapter 7, while Figure 8.1b is furthest from it. Nevertheless, if we examine the structure diagrams in Figures 8.1a, b and c alongside Figure 7.9 (reproduced as Figure 8.2, for convenience), we may note that many of the items in the new structure diagram are more or less the same as the items in the old one. This illustrates one of the major advantages of writing well-structured programs which use procedures. It demonstrates a common enough situation such as this for example, where we have already written procedures which carry out some of the tasks required in a new program. In such a case there is no reason for going back to rewrite the procedures which have already been written. On the contrary, we know that the procedures used in Chapter 7 have already been fully tested and proved to perform the correct tasks accurately. It would therefore be foolish to rewrite and run the risk of introducing additional errors unnecessarily. It is quite sufficient that we should carry out a careful check to ensure that the requirements of the new procedure *really are exactly the same* as those of the old one.

However, the above discussion must be viewed with caution. We must be clear about exactly what is the appropriate stage to identify which of the procedures already written may be used in a new program. In our present example, we have already defined three possible ways of implementing an improved program, and have designed each of these solutions in outline (using a structure diagram). It is appropriate to decide on the 'best' method and *then* to examine whether or not any procedures already written can be used. We must realise the *fundamental importance* of designing the program in *the most appropriate way*, without being influenced by the stock of procedures which we might feel we would want to use. The availability of ready-written and tested procedures must be seen as a bonus, and not as a motive for selecting a particular route to solving the problem!

This can be particularly important in a situation where an existing well-tested computer system requires minor modification. Then it is very tempting to try a simple upgrade based upon fine-tuning and 'patching' of the existing procedures. However, it is a very dangerous route to take because this leads to badly designed, ill thought-out programs which are impossible to maintain later; and the location of bugs during development and testing will be a massive task. The additional time taken to develop a well-planned approach (it may often use a similar proportion of the already prepared material) is time well spent, and will probably save time in the long run.

Therefore, we must now consider which of the three solutions we have identified would seem to be the most appropriate. It is likely to be either solution 8.1a or 8.1c in preference to 8.1b, since either of these gives the customer the opportunity to change selections within an order according to stock availability, whereas option 8.1b does not. In a real programming situation, it would be for management to select which of the alternatives on offer was the most advantageous, basing their judgement on information made available to them by the analyst/programmers. In this instance, we shall look at the solution described in Figure 8.1c since it illustrates a few more techniques than would the Figure 8.1a solution (which is set as an exercise).

Using Figure 8.1c as a guide, we may immediately identify two substantial parts of the program already written which may be retained without amendment. The initial phase where the computer learns about the catalogue goods and price/stock levels needs no changes. Similarly the final phase which produces the management reports need not be changed at all. We may therefore concentrate on the customer processing phase of the program, and in particular, the routine which processes a single customer.

Figure 8.3 gives a detailed breakdown of the processes involved in the program design for dealing with a single customer, and prompts us to identify a large number of procedures from Program 7.10 which will be used here with little or no amendment. The main changes will be to the names of variables and the order in which the procedures are called.

Before we actually begin to put the new customer processing procedure together, we must decide upon a **data structure** to use for storing the details of the order. In the previous chapter we were dealing with a single item at a time. We were therefore able to store just a single catalogue number at a time, together with the two values:

— **Counter,** which stored the index number for the item within the arrays **Catno$( )**, **Desc$( )**, **Price( )**, **Stock( )**, and

— **Quantity** which stored how many of the item were required.

In our new situation, we shall need to be able to store a list of the catalogue numbers of items ordered, alongside the corresponding list of index numbers. We are prompted to use three arrays: **Order$( )** which stores the list of catalogue numbers **(cf Cat$)**, **Index( )** which stores the array indexes for each item required **(cf Counter)**, and **Numberreq( )** which stores the size of the order for each item **(cf Quantity)**.

Note that we have not used the same variable names for the arrays in our new example as we did for the corresponding single variables in the previous chapter. This is a deliberate policy, which will assist us in checking later whether every variable name has been changed when procedures have been taken from the old program for use here.

We shall need to allocate space for these arrays, and we need to choose a size large enough to cope with the number of items which will form the largest possible order. We shall choose to set the array sizes at five for the present, but very simple modifications later would allow this to be changed.

132 BASIC APPLICATIONS

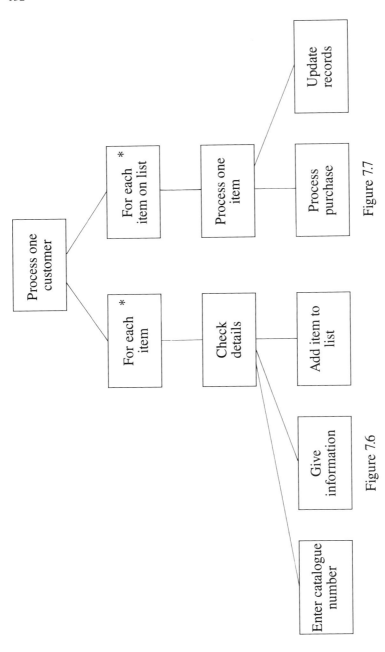

Figure 8.3 Selected Method for Improved Program showing Corresponding Processes from Chapter 7

Exercise A

Look back at Program 7.10 and find an appropriate place to insert DIMension statements for setting up the arrays Order$( ), Index( ) and Numberreq( ), each of size five.

We need to have a way of identifying the end of an individual customer's order if it has fewer than five items on it, and we will do this by specifying that the catalogue number 000/0000 is used after the last item.

We are now in a position to sketch out the overall structure of the procedure for processing one customer (see Figure 8.4).

>   (Input list of items required)
>   Repeat
>   Accept a catalogue number
>   Give information about item
>   Accept quantity required
>   Until either 5 items are accepted or cat. no 000/0000 is input
>   (Process the order)
>   Repeat
>   Print out item on receipt
>   Update records
>   Until either 5 items are processed or cat. no 000/0000 is reached.
>   Print total due on the receipt

Figure 8.4

You will notice that here we have converted the structure diagram (Figure 8.3) into a series of instructions which closely reflect the actual program statements that make up the program we are writing. Here we ignore the details required to make the program technically correct, but can sketch out the overall plan. This enables us to check that the sorts of things we have put onto the structure diagram can be converted into the BASIC statements we intend to use.

In a practical situation, often the most appropriate way to write a program such as this one is to use a large piece of paper and to map out in pencil the outline program in the way we have presented it here. Plenty of space must be left for completing the details later. We may then go through the outline converting descriptions of operations into procedure calls and adding the necessary technical detail. It is important to keep the structure diagram in view while doing this, in order to check that the program developed performs according to the original specification.

Figures 8.5 and 8.6 are provided to illustrate how this program might be developed through two further stages.

(Input list of items required)
Itemno = 1
Repeat
  Accept a catalogue number (put in Order$(Itemno))
  Give information about item (need to locate Order$(Itemno) in Catno$( ) and store in Index(Itemno))
  Accept quantity required (put in Numberreq (Itemno))
  Increase Itemno by 1
Until either 5 items are accepted or cat. no 000/0000 is input
(Process the order)
Itemno = 1
Repeat
  Print out item on receipt
  Update records (need to update stock, total sales and total order value for this customer !!NB Have not set this up yet!!)
Until either 5 items are processed or cat. no 000/0000 is reached.
Print total due on the receipt

Figure 8.5

(Input list of items required)
Thisorder=0
Itemno = 1
Repeat
  Procedure Dataentry # #
  Order$(Itemno)=Cat$
  Procedure Information # #
  Index(Itemno)=Counter
  Procedure Givequantity # #
  Numberreq(Itemno)=Quantity
  Increase Itemno by 1
Until either 5 items are accepted or cat. no 000/0000 is input
(Process the order)
Itemno = 1
Repeat
  !!!New procedure to print receipt!!!
  !!!New procedure update!!!
Until either 5 items are processed or cat. no 000/0000 is reached.
Print *Thisorder* on the receipt

Figure 8.6

Exercise B

Referring to Figure 8.6, write out the program which is being developed here, and see if it will run. If you are having difficulties, try looking at Appendix 3, Program 8.1. (Note: the one area which might cause problems is how to finish the day's transactions. Assume that the final customer is entered as 999/9999 for the first item and 000/0000 as the second item.)

KEEPING TRACK OF STOCK LEVELS

In Chapter 7 we stored our stock levels within the data statements giving details of catalogue numbers, descriptions and prices. This is a rather unsatisfactory thing to do, because while catalogue numbers, prices and descriptions will change only occasionally (ie they are *static* data), the stock levels must be continually updated as items are sold, and new deliveries are received. Making changes to the actual program statements on a regular basis would therefore be necessary if stock is stored in this way. This is time-consuming, because some of the adjustments to stock could be made automatically as items are sold, and might result in changes being made inadvertently elsewhere in the program. Errors may therefore be introduced.

For data items which are continually being updated, it is desirable to have an alternative method of storing the data which can easily be updated. The method which is generally used employs disk **files**. By a file, we simply mean an area of a disk where some items are stored. Thus we may have a *program file* — an area of disk where the instructions of a program are stored for later use, or a *data file* — where data is stored for later use. In the present situation, we shall be concerned with the use of data files.

If you refer to books on file processing, then you will find reference to several different types of file. The type of data file which concerns us here is the *'Serial'* file, which simply means that the data items are stored on the file one after another and can only be read back in the same order. These are the simplest types of file to understand, but for some applications they are very slow and the alternative *'Random access file'* is to be preferred. Unfortunately, not all versions of the BASIC programming language allow the use of random access files.

Our use of files in the catalogue shopping program is very simple. All we need to do is to store the information on stock levels in a disk file rather than within data statements. We shall need to be able to read in the information about stock at the begining of each session (within the initialisation procedure), and write it out to disk at the end of the session, ready for the new day's trading. We must therefore develop techniques for creating a file on disk, and techniques for reading its contents back into the computer.

(a) Creating a new file

Let us imagine that we want to create a disk file containing 10 numbers, by typing the numbers in at the keyboard. There are three stages in the program, and they are illustrated in Figure 8.7. The corresponding program is shown as Programs 8.2a and b. We may use more or less any name we choose for the file. In the example shown, the filename '**File**' has been assumed.

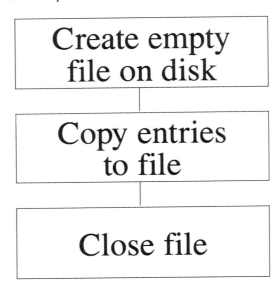

Figure 8.7   Simple File Creation

Program 8.2a (RM BASIC version)

```
10   REM FILE CREATE
20   CREATE # 3, "File"
30   FOR I=1 TO 10
40   PRINT "Type in next number"
50   INPUT X
60   PRINT # 3,X
70   NEXT I
80   CLOSE # 3
```

Program 8.2b (IBM BASICA/Turbo Basic version)

```
10   REM FILE CREATE
20   OPEN "File" FOR OUTPUT AS # 1
```

```
30  FOR I=1 TO 10
40  PRINT "Type in next number"
50  INPUT X
60  PRINT # 1,X
70  NEXT I
80  CLOSE # 1
```

Note: while it is possible to write more than one variable to a single line of a file, this may cause unnecessary complications for the beginner. For this reason, we shall always only send a single variable to a file at a time. Thus:

$$\text{PRINT \# 5, Fred\$}$$

would be acceptable, while:

$$\text{PRINT \# 5,Fred\$,Sam}$$

would not.

(b) Retrieving the old file

Similarly, there are three stages involved in reading the contents of the serial data file created by Programs 8.2a and b into an array List( ) and printing the entries on the screen. These are illustrated in the diagram (see Figure 8.8) and in Programs 8.3a and b.

Program 8.3a (RM BASIC version)

```
 10  REM FILE READ AND DISPLAY
 20  DIM List(10)
 30  OPEN # 4,"File"
 40  FOR I=1 TO 10
 50  INPUT # 4,List(I)
 60  NEXT I
 70  CLOSE # 4
 80  PRINT "Input from disk now complete"
 90  FOR I=1 TO 10
100  PRINT List(I)
110  NEXT I
```

Program 8.3b (IBM BASICA/Turbo Basic version)

```
10  REM FILE READ AND DISPLAY
20  DIM List(10)
30  OPEN "File" FOR INPUT AS #1
40  FOR I=1 TO 10
50  INPUT #1,List(I)
60  NEXT I
```

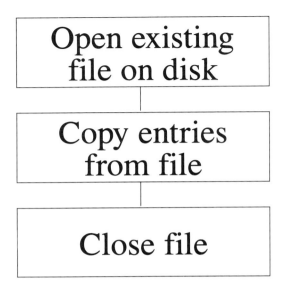

Figure 8.8 Simple File Retrieval

```
 70  CLOSE #1
 80  PRINT "Input from disk now complete"
 90  FOR I=1 TO 10
100  PRINT List(I)
110  NEXT I
```

Notice that in Programs 8.2 and 8.3, we have assumed that we know the size of the file in advance, and therefore the loop which we have used is a count-controlled FOR . . . NEXT loop. In many practical applications it will be equally appropriate to have file access controlled using a condition-controlled loop (REPEAT/WHILE) with the exit condition being satisfied by the final entry in the file. This may often be a 'dummy' entry such as −9999, in the case of a file of numbers, or # # # # in the case of a file of strings.

(c) Changing the file contents

We shall frequently find ourselves in the situation where we have a file already stored on disk but need to change it. This will be the situation at the end of each day's operation of the catalogue program since the stock levels will need to be updated. Unfortunately, with serial files there is generally no way of changing the contents of a file directly. Instead, the old file must be renamed and a new file created by copying the entries from the old to the new, making any necessary changes to each entry before it is written to the new file. For this reason, only file creation and file retrieval need concern us here, since updating is a combination of these two operations. Standard books on data processing give detailed consideration to the question of serial and sequential file processing; they describe algorithms (methods) which are generally applicable in a data processing situation and which may be translated into programs for these tasks.

The *overall* design of the catalogue program does not need to be changed at all simply in order to use files. We shall only need to change two procedures:

Initialise, so that the final column of DATA is no longer used for the Stock( ) array, but this information is instead obtained from the disk file '**Stockfile**', and:

Stocklist, which must be amended to create a new Stockfile for the next day.

Where possible, we shall preserve the previous day's Stockfile under the title '**Oldstock**' to reflect good data processing practice. In the event of a disaster causing the day's data to be lost, we would be able to use the **Oldstock** file as an alternative to having to abandon the entire system, even though it would obviously result in the use of incorrect stock levels.

Stock deliveries will need to be covered in a separate program. For simplicity we shall use a simple data entry program (similar to Programs 8.2a and b) for the creation of an initial Stockfile, and for the creation of a new Stockfile after each new delivery of goods. An exercise is set for the reader to incorporate a facility within the main program, which allows for a catalogue number to be entered along with the size of a delivery, and increases the stock level accordingly.

Programs 8.4a, b, c, d, and e list the new procedures Initialise and Stocklist.

Program 8.4a

Procedure Initialise (RM BASIC version)

```
1000   PROCEDURE Initialise
1005   GLOBAL Desc$( ),Catno$( ),Price( ),Stock( )
1010   DIM Desc$(10),Catno$(10),Price(10),Stock(10)
1020   FOR I=1 TO 10
1030   READ Catno$(I),Desc$(I),Price(I)
1040   NEXT I
1050   DATA "100/1111";"Teddy bear",5.99
1060   DATA "101/2213";"Radio",17.99
```

(Note: your program will need ten DATA lines which should include the ten items which you wish to sell.)

```
1150    OPEN # 4, "Stockfile"
1160    FOR I=1 TO 10
1170    INPUT # 4,Stock(I)
1180    NEXT I
1190    CLOSE # 4
1200    ENDPROC
```

Program 8.4b

Procedure Initialise (Turbo Basic version)

```
1000    SUB Initialise
1005    SHARED Desc$( ),Catno$( ),Price( ),Stock( )
1010    DIM Desc$(10),Catno$(10),Price(10),Stock(10)
1020    FOR I=1 TO 10
1030    READ Catno$(I),Desc$(I),Price(I)
1040    NEXT I
1050    DATA "100/1111";"Teddy bear", 5.99
1060    DATA "101/2213";"Radio",17.99
```

(Note: your program will need ten DATA lines which should include the ten items which you wish to sell.)

```
1150    OPEN "Stockfile" FOR INPUT AS # 1
1160    FOR I=1 TO 10
1170    INPUT # 1, Stock(I)
1180    NEXT I
1190    CLOSE # 1
1200    END SUB
```

Program 8.4c

Procedure Initialise (IBM BASICA)

```
1000    REM Read in data to arrays
1010    DIM Desc$(10),Catno$(10),Price(10),Stock(10)
1020    FOR I=1 TO 10
1030    READ Catno$(I),Desc$(I),Price(I)
1040    NEXT I
1050    DATA "100/1111";"Teddy bear",5.99
1060    DATA "101/2213";"Radio",17.99
```

(Note: your program will need ten DATA lines which should include the ten items which you wish to sell.)

```
1150    OPEN "Stockfile" FOR INPUT AS #1
1160    FOR I=1 TO 10
1170    INPUT    1,Stock(I)
1180    NEXT I
```

```
1190  CLOSE #1
1200  RETURN
```

Program 8.4d

Procedure Stocklist (RM BASIC version)

```
3200  PROCEDURE Stocklist
3210  GLOBAL Stock( ),Catno$( ),Desc$( )
3220  RENAME "Stockfile";"Oldstock"
3230  CREATE #3, "Stockfile"
3240  FOR I=1 TO 10
3250  PRINT Catno$(I),Desc$(I),Stock(I)
3260  PRINT #3,Stock(I)
3270  NEXT I
3280  CLOSE #3
3290  ENDPROC
```

Program 8.4e

Procedure Stocklist (Turbo Basic version)

```
3200  SUB Stocklist
3210  SHARED Stock( ),Catno$( ),Desc$( )
3220  OPEN "Stockfile" FOR OUTPUT AS #1
3230  FOR I=1 TO 10
3240  PRINT Catno$(I),Desc$(I),Stock(I)
3250  PRINT #1,Stock(I)
3260  NEXT I
3270  CLOSE #1
3280  END SUB
```

Note: the IBM BASICA version of procedure Stocklist is identical to the Turbo Basic version, except for the absence of the SUB and SHARED instructions, and the replacement of the END SUB by RETURN as usual.

Exercise C

Make the above amendments to the program from Chapter 7 and check that it will run. Make a list of any features which you consider to be unsatisfactory, and see whether you are able to solve any of the problems.

Exercise D

Incorporate additional procedures which allow for *delivered* goods to be *added* to the stock records from within the main program.

DAILY PERFORMANCE RECORDS

It is common for computerised systems to keep details of day-by-day performance on file for monthly analysis. Here we shall develop a procedure which creates a file containing the values of total sales for each day of operation; this may then be integrated with our existing program.

This requirement seems very simple: all we need to do is to store the date and the value of Totsales for each day in a disk file. Unfortunately, as we discussed earlier, it is not possible to add an extra entry or two to a file which has already been created. Instead, it is necessary to create a new file which contains all the old entries together with the additional new ones. The overall plan is shown in Figure 8.9, and a structure diagram illustrating the solution is given in Figure 8.10.

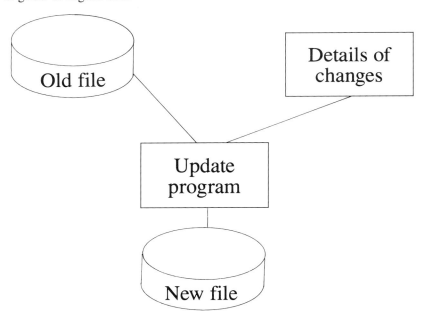

Figure 8.9 Schematic Diagram for File Update

The detailed solution is given in Programs 8.5a, b and c. Note the use of the entries −999 and # # # for the total sales and date, respectively, of the dummy entries within the file. These allow the end of file to be detected even though the number of existing entries within the file is unknown. Note also how the program assumes the existence of a file before it is run. It is therefore essential that a simple file with an appropriate structure eg 1 Date, 1 Value, # # # , −999) is set up before the initial use of the program shown here.

CAN I HELP YOU AGAIN? 143

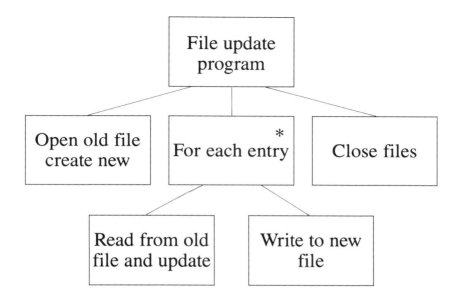

Figure 8.10 File Update Structure Diagram

Program 8.5a.

Procedure to update day-by-day summary (RM BASIC version)

```
PROCEDURE Salessummary
GLOBAL Totsales
RENAME "Salesrec", " Oldrec"
OPEN # 3,"Oldrec"
CREATE # 4,"Salesrec"
REPEAT
INPUT # 3,D$
INPUT # 3,Sales
IF D$<>" # # #" THEN PRINT # 4,D$:PRINT #4,Sales
UNTIL D$=" # # # "
PRINT # 4,Date$
PRINT # 4,Totsales
PRINT # 4," # # # "
PRINT # 4,-999
CLOSE # 3
CLOSE # 4
ENDPROC
```

Note: the use of Date$ which contains the current date, and the IF statements which prevent us from writing the dummy terminating entries to the file before the new entry.

Program 8.5b Turbo Basic

```
SUB Salessummary
SHARED Totsales
OPEN "Oldrec" FOR OUTPUT AS #1
OPEN "Salesrec" FOR INPUT AS #2
DO
INPUT #2,D$
INPUT #2,Sales
PRINT #1,D$
PRINT #1,Sales
UNTIL D$=" # # # "
CLOSE #1
CLOSE #2
OPEN "Oldrec" FOR INPUT AS #1
OPEN "Salesrec" FOR OUTPUT AS #2
DO
INPUT #1,D$
INPUT #1,Sales
IF D$<> " # # # " THEN PRINT #2,D$:PRINT #2,Sales
UNTIL D$=" # # # "
PRINT #2,Date$
PRINT #2,Totsales
PRINT #2," # # # "
PRINT #2,-999
CLOSE #2
CLOSE #1
END SUB
```

Note: the Salesrec file must initially be copied to Oldrec instead of using the RENAME command available with RM BASIC. In fact RENAME is a mixed blessing, because although the operation is faster, any failure will result in loss of the existing file contents. In contrast the copying process used in the Turbo Basic version does not suffer as much from this danger, since it works on two separate copies of the file.

Program 8.5c IBM BASICA version

```
REM Sales summary procedure
OPEN "Oldrec" FOR OUTPUT AS #1
OPEN "Salesrec" for INPUT AS #2
D$=" "
```

```
WHILE D$<>" # # # "
INPUT #2,D$
INPUT #2,Sales
PRINT #1,D$
PRINT #1,Sales
WEND
CLOSE #1
CLOSE #2
OPEN "Oldrec" FOR INPUT AS #1
OPEN "Salesrec" FOR OUTPUT AS #2
D$= " "
WHILE D$<>" # # #"
INPUT #1,D$
INPUT #1,Sales
IF D$<>" # # # " THEN PRINT #2,D$: PRINT #2,Sales
WEND
PRINT #2,Date$
PRINT #2,Totsales
PRINT #2," # # # "
PRINT #2,-999
CLOSE #2
CLOSE #1
RETURN
```

Note: in this case, the use of the WHILE/WEND construction necessitates the additional D$=" " commands to give D$ an appropriate initial value before the loop is entered.

Exercise E

Write a program which creates a suitable initial "Salesrec" file as discussed above, and a second simple program which reads the contents of a "Salesrec" file one by one and prints each on the screen.

Exercise F

Integrate the Sales record procedure described here into your main program. Run the program for several days, and then see whether the program developed in Exercise E finds the expected total sales value stored for each day in the file Salesrec.

Note: Exercises E and F illustrate the sorts of processes which are commonly required in order to test programs that are under development. Thus, in Exercise E we have developed programs which may be used to test the behaviour of the main program by examining the files which it creates.

Exercise G*

Try to write a program which sets up a telephone number list. You will need to create a file which stores a list of names and telephone numbers, and have a second program which allows you to type in a name and searches through the file to see whether the correct number is there.

SUMMARY

In this chapter we have applied two fundamental data structures — arrays and files — to the program developed in Chapter 7, in order to give a more realistic performance. The techniques of sequential file processing introduced here are important in a substantial proportion of application programs.

---

*This question is more advanced and may be left until later if you wish.

9 A Mathematical Diversion

INTRODUCTION

In this chapter we shall discuss two particular examples which have a mathematical nature, but are also of general interest. We shall also briefly meet the range of mathematical functions which are readily available to the BASIC programmer.

In the first example, we shall simulate the throwing of two dice, and produce a simple block graph showing the number of occurrences of each possible total score in fifty throws. The second example will concern the drawing on screen of a graph for a standard mathematical function.

SIMULATIONS

Where the results of an experiment are needed, but the experiment would be too dangerous or too expensive to perform, a method of *simulating* the actual experiment is sought. Scientists sometimes use scale models to do this, but recently the use of computer simulations has become very common. As long as we are able to express some relationship between the likelihood of different possible outcomes, it may be possible to produce a reasonable simulation of an experiment on a computer.

As a simple example, we will consider the wish to record the outcomes of an experiment involving throwing two dice on fifty separate occasions. The frequencies of the possible combined scored will then be represented using a block graph. Obviously, in this case, it would be perfectly simple to perform the experiment in practice, therefore the simulation has little immediate practical value. However, if the number of dice throws was increased to 5000, then the actual performance of the experiment would be much less attractive than the simulation.

We may express the outline solution to this problem as shown in Figure 9.1. Clearly the program naturally divides into two main sections: the dice throwing section and the graph drawing section. We shall consider these two sections in greater detail.

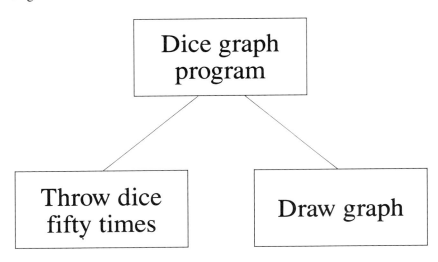

Figure 9.1 Outline Design for Dice Simulation Program

But first we will need to decide on the storage of the data, which in this case refers to the frequency with which each of the possible total scores 2,3, . . . ,12 occurs. It makes sense to store these values in an array called **Frequency( )**, and this will need to be *initialised* to zero before it may be used. We will also need to determine how a particular throw of the dice may be generated by the computer.

Pseudo-random Numbers

Because of the desire to use computers to simulate real-life situations, and the requirement to build into these simulations some element of chance, many computer languages supply some method of generating 'random' numbers. By a *'random number generator'* we mean a command which we may use to provide us with a number of a particular type, chosen by the computer in such a way that we cannot easily predict what number the computer will select. Commonly, these random number generators supply a fraction between 0 and 1 which may then be used within a program, together with an appropriate conversion routine,

A MATHEMATICAL DIVERSION

to provide a random value of a more suitable type.

These 'random numbers' are more correctly termed *'pseudo-random numbers'*, due to the fact that they are generated by the computer using a carefully designed formula, which the computer user will not usually be aware of. The computer is not, in fact, generating the numbers at random, although they will appear random to the user. The actual formula used by the computer to generate these random numbers must be designed very carefully to ensure that there is no bias in the numbers which are generated.

In our present example, we shall wish to generate a whole number between 1 and 6 for each die and then add these together to give the total score. We use the function RND(1) to generate the initial random number for each die in the example shown in Program 9.1.

Program 9.1

```
X=RND(1)
Y=RND(1)
Die1=INT(6*X + 1)
Die2=INT(6*Y + 1)
Score=Die1+Die2
```

Note in this example, how the function INT is used. INT allows the conversion between numbers with a fractional part and the whole number obtained by deleting the fractional part. The numbers X and Y will be fractions between 0 and 1, and are multiplied by 6 to give numbers between 0 and 6. By adding 1, the results lie between 1 and 7, so that deleting the fractional part using INT leaves a whole number which is 1, 2, 3, 4, 5 or 6 as required. To illustrate this more clearly, the calculation for X=0.678 is shown below.

X=0.678
so 6*X=4.068
and INT(6*X+1)=5.

Note that INT simply throws away the fractional part of the number given in the brackets following it and does not perform 'rounding' in the traditional way.

Figure 9.2 represents a refinement of Figure 9.1 which illustrates in more detail how the program will be structured. You will observe that the requirement for 50 dice throws lends itself to a simple count-controlled loop construction, and that within the main loop there will simply be the code required to evaluate the current dice throws (as in Program 9.1), and to increase the appropriate element of the array Frequency( ) by 1. Program 9.2 gives all the necessary statements to accomplish the first part of the main program.

Program 9.2

```
REM Initialisation
DIM Frequency(12)
FOR I=1 TO 12
Frequency(I)=0
NEXT I
REM Dice Throws
FOR J=1 TO 50
X=RND(1)
Y=RND(1)
Die1=INT(6*X+1)
Die2=INT(6*Y+1)
Score=Die1+Die2
Frequency(Score)=Frequency(Score)+1
NEXT J
```

Exercise A

Rewrite the program lines from Program 9.2 using procedures which more accurately reflect the overall design of the solution as illustrated in Figure 9.2. (Note: you will need to use GLOBAL/SHARED statements as appropriate to your version of BASIC.)

PRODUCING A BLOCK GRAPH

The program segment which we shall require for drawing a block graph is in fact remarkably simple to write. In order to illustrate the principle involved, Figure 9.3 illustrates the appearance of a typical block graph for this program.

We shall need to draw the axes, mark on the scales, and finally produce the blocks. Drawing the axes simply requires the use of the line-drawing graphics facilities, and we may then mark the scales using the standard techniques for adding text to a diagram. The remaining task is to produce the blocks.

The most difficult part of producing the blocks has nothing to do with writing computer programs, but involves adapting the scale chosen to represent frequency on the screen to give the actual co-ordinates of the corners of the box we need to draw. We will now discuss the stages in detail.

Figure 9.4a shows the graph from Figure 9.3 superimposed on the screen co-ordinates from RM BASIC in mode 80, and Figure 9.4b shows the corresponding situation in Turbo/IBM BASIC set to screen mode 2. Once we have these co-ordinates to hand, we may easily produce segments of program which draw the axes and mark on the scales. This is an easy task since these are fixed and involve only the use of line-drawing facilities and writing text in the appropriate positions (see Programs 9.3a and b).

A MATHEMATICAL DIVERSION

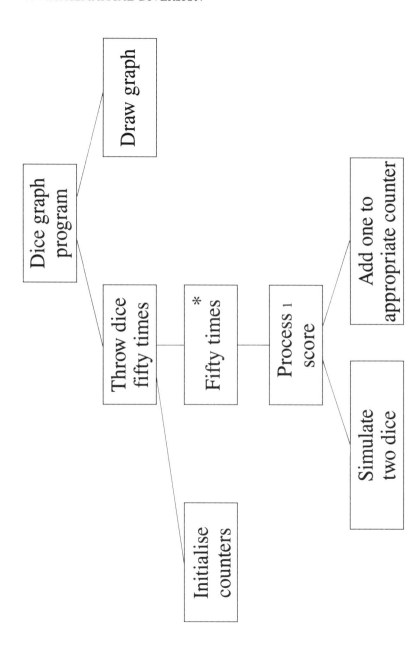

Figure 9.2 More Detailed Design for Dice Simulation Program

152   BASIC APPLICATIONS

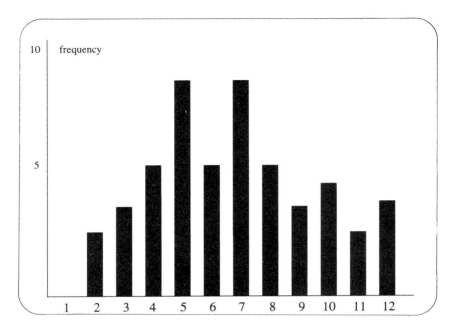

Figure 9.3   Typical Appearance of Block Graph on Screen

Program 9.3a (RM BASIC)

**LINE 10,20;630,20
LINE 20,10;20,240
PLOT "Frequency";10,240
PLOT "10";10,220
PLOT "5";10,120
PLOT "1";50,10
PLOT "2";100,10
PLOT "3";150,10**
(and so on)

Program 9.3b (IBM)

**LINE (10,180)−(630,180)
LINE (20,190)−(20,10)
LOCATE (1,1) : PRINT "Frequency"
LOCATE (1,4) : PRINT "10"
LOCATE (24,7) : PRINT "1"**

A MATHEMATICAL DIVERSION

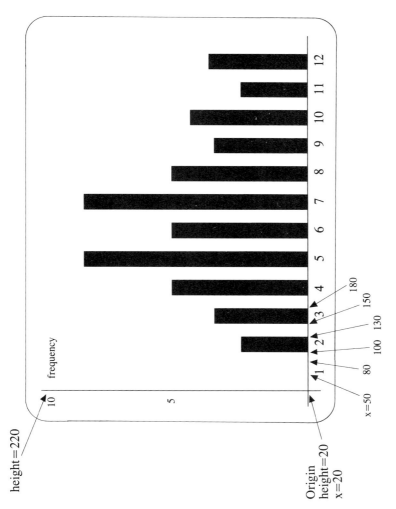

Figure 9.4a RM BASIC Screen Co-ordinates for Graph

154 BASIC APPLICATIONS

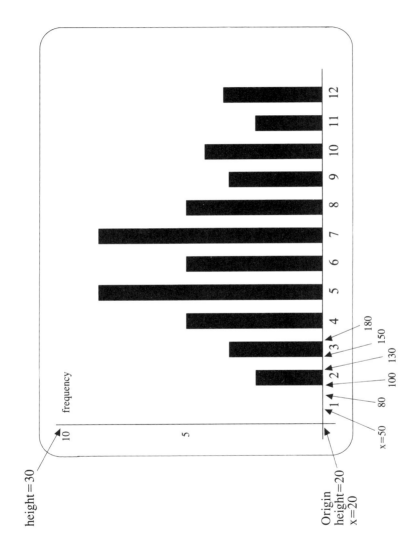

Figure 9.4b IBM Screen Co-ordinates for Graph

A MATHEMATICAL DIVERSION

```
LOCATE (24,13) : PRINT "2"
LOCATE (24,19) : PRINT "3"
```

(and so on — you will need to experiment to get the co-ordinates exactly correct).

In order to draw each block, we shall need to consider the two variations of BASIC separately.

RM BASIC

For each block we shall need an AREA command which lists the four corners of the block. From Figure 9.4a we can see the values of the co-ordinates of the *bottom* corners of each block, and we also know the *x co-ordinates* of the corresponding top corners (since these will be the same as for the bottom corners of the same block). The remaining task is to calculate the y co-ordinates.

Notice that the level of the x-axis (ie frequency = 0) is at height 20 on the screen, and the position of frequency=10 on the scale is at height 220. The scale in use is therefore 20 screen units for each one frequency, and the screen value for a frequency **F** must therefore be 20+20*F (ie go up to level 20 where the graph starts, and then count up the frequency in 20s). This is all we need to know, since the first block may now be drawn using the command:

AREA 50,20;80,20;80,20+20*Frequency(1);50,20+20*Frequency(1)

Naturally, this particular block will have a frequency of zero, since it is not possible to score a total of 1 on two dice! It is now a simple exercise to complete the remaining eleven blocks, each using a separate AREA statement. The details are given in Program 9.4a.

Program 9.4a

AREA 50,20;80,20;80,20+20*Frequency(1);50,20+20*Frequency(1)
AREA 100,20;130,20;130,20+20*Frequency(2);100,20+20*Frequency(2)
AREA 150,20;180,20;180,20+20*Frequency(3);150,20+20*Frequency(3)
AREA 200,20;230,20;230,20+20*Frequency(4);200,20+20*Frequency(4)
AREA 250,20;280,20;280,20+20*Frequency(5);250,20+20*Frequency(5)
AREA 300,20;330,20;330,20+20*Frequency(6);300,20+20*Frequency(6)
AREA 350,20;380,20;380,20+20*Frequency(7);350,20+20*Frequency(7)
AREA 400,20;430,20;430,20+20*Frequency(8);400,20+20*Frequency(8)
AREA 450,20;480,20;480,20+20*Frequency(9);450,20+20*Frequency(9)
AREA 500,20;530,20;530,20+20*Frequency(10);500,20+20*Frequency(10)
AREA 550,20;580,20;580,20+20*Frequency(11);550,20+20*Frequency(11)
AREA 600,20;630,20;630,20+20*Frequency(12);600,20+20*Frequency(12)

IBM BASICs

For the IBM BASICs, we shall need to draw each block using a series of **LINE** commands followed by a **PAINT** command. In essence this is broadly similar to that discussed above for RM BASIC, but it is worth filling in the details here because of the subtle differences in the screen display.

We must remember at all times that the IBM y co-ordinates increase as we move *down* the screen. This is slightly inconvenient, since we are accustomed to using co-ordinates which increase as we move upwards. Therefore in all graph work we need to be careful not to finish up with all the graphs upside down!

The screen shown in Figure 9.4b has the x-axis drawn at the 180 level, and the value for frequency 10 is marked on the scale at level 30. The scale which we are using is thus 15 screen co-ordinates for every single frequency step, and so the position which we must choose to represent a frequency of F is given by the following expression: 180−15*F. The minus sign reflects the 'upside-down' nature of the screen co-ordinate system which we are using.

We are therefore in a position to draw the boxes. The code required to draw the first block is as follows:

```
LINE (50,180)−(80,180)
LINE −(80,180−15*Frequency(1))
LINE −(50,180−15*Frequency(1))
LINE −(50,180)
IF Frequency(1)<>0 THEN PAINT (65,170),CLOR
```

The IF condition is necessary in the PAINT line to avoid shading in the background in the event that the frequency was zero and therefore the point with y=170 in the PAINT command would lie outside of the block drawn.

It is now a simple task to complete the graph-drawing part of the program by writing a further eleven similar segments of code, one for each of the remaining blocks on the graph. The details are given in Program 9.4b.

Program 9.4b

```
LINE (50,180)−(80,180)
LINE −(80,180−15*Frequency(1))
LINE −(50,180−15*Frequency(1))
LINE −(50,180)
IF Frequency(1)<>0 THEN PAINT(65,170),CLOR
LINE (100,180)−(130,180)
LINE −(130,180−15*Frequency(2))
LINE −(100,180−15*Frequency(2))
LINE −(100,180)
IF Frequency(2)<>0 THEN PAINT(115,170),CLOR
LINE (150,180)−(180,180)
LINE −(180,180−15*Frequency(3))
LINE −(150,180−15*Frequency(3))
LINE −(150,180)
```

```
IF Frequency(3)<>0 THEN PAINT (165,170),CLOR
LINE (200,180)-(230,180)
LINE -(230,180-15*Frequency(4))
LINE -(200,180-15*Frequency(4))
LINE -(200,180)
IF Frequency(4)<>0 THEN PAINT(215,170),CLOR
LINE (250,180)-(280,180)
LINE -(280,180-15*Frequency(5))
LINE -(250,180-15*Frequency(5))
LINE -(250,180)
IF Frequency(5)<>0 THEN PAINT(265,170),CLOR
LINE (300,180)-(330,180)
LINE -(330,180-15*Frequency(6))
LINE -(300,180-15*Frequency(6))
LINE -(300,180)
IF Frequency(6)<>0 THEN PAINT(315,170),CLOR
LINE (350,180)-(380,180)
LINE -(380,180-15*Frequency(7))
LINE -(350,180-15*Frequency(7))
LINE -(350,180)
IF Frequency(7)<>0 THEN PAINT(365,170),CLOR
LINE (400,180)-(430,180)
LINE -(430,180-15*Frequency(8))
LINE -(400,180-15*Frequency(8))
LINE -(400,180)
IF Frequency(8)<>THEN PAINT(415,170),CLOR
LINE (450,180)-(480,180)
LINE -(480,180-15*Frequency(9))
LINE -(450,180-15*Frequency(9))
LINE -(450,180)
IF Frequency(9)<>0 THEN PAINT(465,170),CLOR
LINE (500,180)-(530,180)
LINE -(530,180-15*Frequency(10))
LINE -(500,180-15*Frequency(10))
LINE -(500,180)
IF Frequency(10)<>0 THEN PAINT(515,170),CLOR
LINE (550,180)-(580,180)
LINE -(580,180-15*Frequency(11))
LINE -(550,180-15*Frequency(11))
LINE -(550,180)
IF Frequency(11)<>0 THEN PAINT(565,170),CLOR
LINE (600,180)-(630,180)
LINE -(630,180-15*Frequency(12))
```

```
        LINE  -(600,180-15*Frequency(12))
        LINE  -(600,180)
        IF Frequency(12)<>0 THEN PAINT(615,170),CLOR
```

Exercise B

Write a complete program to simulate the dice throwing and produce the graph of the frequencies of each score. You may like to consider extending your program to make a rather more effective display while the initial dice throwing simulation is going on. Try writing some procedures which produce the images of dice on the screen showing different numbers of dots, and integrate these procedures into your simulation so that each number thrown is shown in turn by two dice illustrated on the screen.

Exercise C

Write a program which allows the results of a survey of the colours of 25 cars to be stored in an array and represented using a block graph.

DRAWING A CURVE

We have already discussed in this chapter several of the issues which we shall need to consider when we want to draw the graph of a curve described by a mathematical function. For the present example, we will draw the curve representing the function $y=x^2+5x+1$ for values of x between 0 and 5.

Those who are familiar with this type of task will readily observe that when x takes values between 0 and 5, y will take values between 1 and 51, which prompts the selection of the basic axes shown in Figure 9.5. If you are not familiar with this then do not worry, we have simply selected numbers which avoid the graph going over the edge of the screen.

In order to draw a curve given by an expression, as in this example, we must take a set of values for x and calculate (using the expression given) the corresponding values of y, and then plot the points on the graph, joining each to its neighbour. In theory, we should use a curved line to join the points together, but in practice we shall join them using straight lines, and assume that because we choose the values of x to be very close together, the appearance of the graph will be acceptable.

We may now summarise the method which we will be using in the structure diagram in Figure 9.6.

Using mode 80 in RM BASIC and screen mode 2 on an IBM, we have the horizontal screen co-ordinates taking values from 0 to 639. If we take a screen value of 50 to be x=0, and then put x=1 at screen value of 150, x=2 at 250, and so on so that x=5 is at 550, then we shall have a suitable scale along the x-axis. The relationship is as follows:

A MATHEMATICAL DIVERSION

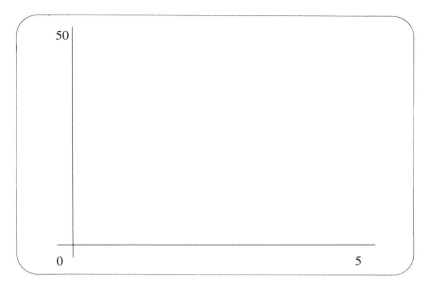

Figure 9.5 Basic Axes for Curve Sketch

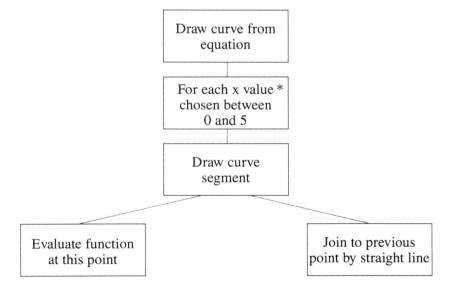

Figure 9.6 Structure Diagram for the Curve Drawing Program

$$ScreenX = 50 + X*100$$

(**Note:** in general, the relationship would be:

$$ScreenX = Startingvalue + X*Stepsize)$$

For the y values, if we draw the x-axis across at level 20 from the bottom (ie 20 on RM BASIC, 180 on IBM), and use a scale of 3 screen units to 1 y value, then the graph will fit comfortably on the screen. Again we have the simple relationships:

$$RMScreenY = 20 + 3*Y$$
$$IBMScreenY = 180 - 3*Y$$

With this information to hand, drawing the curve will be relatively straightforward once we have evaluated the required (x, y) points using the equation. In order to do this, we shall define a function. In other words, we shall teach the computer the relationship between the value of one variable (x) and the other variable (y). This is done using the BASIC statement:

$$DEF\ FNY(X) = X^2 + 5*X + 1$$

When we use a DEF FN statement like this one in a program, we may then use the function FNY elsewhere and the computer will refer back to the definition <> to find out what it means. The setting up of a function is therefore broadly similar to the definition of a part of a program as a procedure. It allows us to set up a particular instruction or group of instructions which we shall need elsewhere and refer to it by name whenever we need it. In most of the situations *outside mathematical applications* we shall find procedures more useful than functions, and it is for this reason that we have discussed these in greater detail and at an earlier stage.

We are now in a position to write the part of the program which actually draws the graph. This is given in Program 9.5.

Program 9.5

    DEF FNY(X)=X*X+5*X+1
    Stepsize=0.5
    Startx=50
    Starty=23 (Starty = 177)
    FOR X=0 TO 50 STEP Stepsize
    Y=FNY(X)
    ScreenX=50+X*100
  [**RMScreenY=INT(20+3*Y)**]   select
     IBMScreenY=INT(180−3*Y)   appropriate
  [**LINE Startx,Starty;ScreenX,RMScreenY**]
     LINE (Startx,Starty)−(ScreenX,IBMScreenY)
    Startx=ScreenX

A MATHEMATICAL DIVERSION

Starty=RMScreenY   **(Starty=IBMScreenY)**
NEXT X

At first glance, this program looks rather more complicated than we might have expected. However, the only real complication is the use of the variables StartX and StartY which are required to give the starting point for each line which is drawn. This accounts for the initialisation of StartX to 50 and StartY to 23 (or 177) which are the screen co-ordinates corresponding to the point (0,1), the starting point for the curve. After each line segment is drawn the values of StartX and StartY are then updated to the current values of ScreenX and ScreenY in readiness for the next line segment to be added. We have also used the INT instruction to ensure that only whole number co-ordinates are given to the LINE instruction.

The use of the variable Stepsize gives us a valuable control over the graph which is drawn. We have not previously used the STEP option within FOR loops. STEP allows us to specify that the loop counter will not increase by one each time through the loop but instead increases by the number specified by the Stepsize given after the word STEP. In many counting applications, it would be inappropriate to use any alternative stepsize, but occasionally, as in this example, it is desirable to be able to increase by a fraction. As written above, the program will evaluate y at the values of x in the list 0, 0.5, 1.0, 1.5, 2.0, 2.5, 3.0, 3.5, 4.0, 4.5, and 5.0. You can see how the stepsize of 0.5 specifies the gap between the values of x which are used.

Now we must consider whether the choice of Stepsize=0.5 is appropriate. The larger the stepsize, the less work the computer does when calculating and drawing, and therefore the quicker the output is produced. However, with a large stepsize, the straight lines used to join the points together will be clearly straight, and it is possible that they may straighten out some shape of interest in the curve which should have been drawn. On the other hand, with a small stepsize, such as Stepsize=0.001, we might find the curve produced is beautifully smooth and accurate, but takes too long to draw because the computer has to work out values at so many points. It is therefore up to the programmer to decide on a compromise position which gives acceptable accuracy without resulting in excessive delays.

Exercise D

Take the code given in Program 9.5 and use it to produce a procedure for drawing the curve with the equation $y=x^2+5x+1$. Integrate the procedure into a suitable program and experiment to find a suitable stepsize to reach the compromise between speed and accuracy which we discussed above. (Note: your main program will need to set the computer into the suitable screen mode and draw and label the axes, in addition to including the procedure instructions in Program 9.5.)

Exercise E

Rewrite the program from Exercise D so that the graph drawn is for the equation $y=3x^2$ for x varying from 0 to 3 and y from 0 to 30.

Exercise F

Rewrite the program from Exercise D so that the computer draws the graph for $y=x^3-3$ for x varying from 0 to 5, and y from -5 to 80.

PREDEFINED FUNCTIONS

Users who are particularly interested in mathematical applications will require standard mathematical functions such as sines, cosines, square roots and modulus. These are typically provided in BASICs by supplying a number of predefined functions. A selection of these are listed below, but the interested reader should refer to a detailed programmer's reference guide for the particular version of BASIC in use.

Typical function name	Purpose
SIN(X)	Sine function
COS(X)	Cosine function
TAN(X)	Tangent function
ATN(X)	Arctangent function (Inverse tangent)
ABS(X)	Absolute value (modulus)
SQR(X)	Square root
INT(X)	Integer part function
EXP(X)	Exponential function
LOG(X)	Natural logarithm

Exercise G *(for mathematically inclined readers only)*

Use some of the predefined functions listed above within your DEF FNY(X) statement to allow curves involving standard mathematical functions to be drawn using the previous program.

SUMMARY

This chapter has introduced a variety of techniques and facilities related to simulations and graph drawing. Ideas similar to these are applicable in many real applications when a graphical output of the results of a program is needed. However the rest of the book does not depend on the understanding of this chapter, so that readers who may have struggled with it should still be able to progress steadily.

10 More Advanced Topics

INTRODUCTION

In this chapter we shall meet a number of ideas which have not been encountered elsewhere. It will not always be possible to give a full discussion of the techniques described here, but their applications are outlined and the interested reader is directed to more advanced works.

TWO-DIMENSIONAL ARRAYS

The arrays which we have used in earlier chapters have allowed us to store a *list* of items all of the same type, for example a list of names or a list of numbers. These are one-dimensional arrays. Two-dimensional arrays allow us to store a *table*, but once again, all the items within the table must be of the same underlying data type.

To illustrate the use of a two-dimensional array, we shall set up a table which contains the calculation of the mean (or average) based upon the frequencies of scoring the numbers 1, 2, 3, 4, 5 and 6 on throwing a die a number of times. A mathematician would represent the calculation in a table such as Figure 10.1.

How would we structure our method if we were doing this by hand? We would probably begin by taking a large enough piece of paper, sketching out where the columns would go, and then filling in the entries in columns 1 and 2. The values in column 3 may then be easily calculated, and finally the totals of columns 2 and 3 may be evaluated and used to determine the final answer. We shall follow this same order of operations (shown in Figure 10.2) in the computer program.

In order to write a program to solve this problem, we will need a table with 6 rows by 3 columns. This is set up using the command:

DIM Table(6,3)

We can then read the first two columns from DATA statements using the program segment:

Score	Frequency	Score × Frequency
1	12	12
2	15	30
3	9	27
4	11	44
5	12	60
6	8	48
Totals	67	221

Mean = 221/67 = 3.299

Figure 10.1

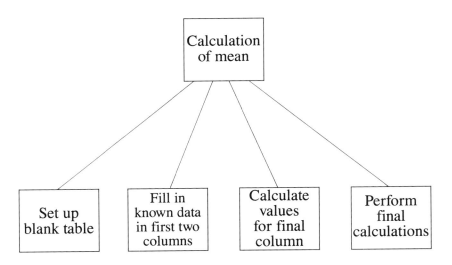

Figure 10.2 Structure Diagram Giving Design for Mean Calculating Program

MORE ADVANCED TOPICS

```
FOR I=1 TO 6
READ Table(I,1)
READ Table(I,2)
NEXT I
DATA 1,12,2,15,3,9,4,11,5,12,6,8
```

The values of column three may then be found using the program instructions:

```
FOR I=1 TO 6
Table(I,3)=Table(I,1)*Table(I,2)
NEXT I
```

To find the column totals we could use a program segment like this:

```
Col2=0
Col3=0
FOR I=1 TO 6
Col2=Col2+Table(I,2)
Col3=Col3+Table(I,3)
NEXT I
```

Finally the answer may be calculated:

Answer=Col3/Col2

The tidying up of the program to actually display the tables on the screen in the required form, and to print out the answer is set as an exercise.

Exercise A

As a follow-up exercise, look at Figure 10.3, which shows the table used to find the 'standard deviation'. Write a computer program which accepts the first two columns from DATA statements and produces the entire table.

Score	Frequency	Score*Frequency	Score*Score*Frequency
1	12	12	12
2	15	30	60
3	9	27	81
4	11	44	176
5	12	60	300
6	8	48	288
Totals	67	221	917
	(Col2)	(Col3)	(Col4)

The answer = Square root of $(Col4/Col2 - \{Col3/Col2\}^2)$

Figure 10.3

RANDOM ACCESS AND INDEXED FILES

When we used files briefly in Chapter 8, we restricted our considerations to serial and sequential files, which simply hold the items of data one after another. They do this in such a way that each item can only be accessed by reading in all the items before it one-by-one. In addition, changes to these files are not normally possible, so an update procedure usually involves renaming the old version of the file and creating a new amended version.

For many modern computer uses, these types of files would be totally inappropriate because they would be far too slow. If a large database of several thousand entries was processed sequentially for on-line enquiries (that is, the information about any entry may be requested and should be available quickly), delays of several minutes or even longer would be inevitable. For this reason alternative methods of access have been developed. In order to use these more sophisticated file processing methods, it is essential to ensure that the version of the computer language in use supports them!

File handling is not generally regarded as BASIC's strong point, and certainly for the most sophisticated file processing applications it would be sensible to choose an alternative language, such as COBOL. However, some modern BASICs do allow for either random or indexed sequential file access.

For **indexed sequential** access, the data on file is stored in sequence as it would be for normal sequential file processing. However, an index is also stored which specifies whereabouts on the disk particular key records are stored. It is therefore possible to search the index for the nearest entry *before the one required* and then start searching the file from that point. The advantage is that, depending on the size of the index in use, a much smaller number of items need be searched before locating the one required. Ideally, indexed sequential files should be updated in a similar way to normal sequential files but some sophisticated methods have been devised which allow for additional entries to be added within the file — usually at the expense of some of the speed of access.

Random files are files which allow (at least in theory) the retrieval of any data item within the file, in a length of time that is independent of the position of the item within the file. This involves a method of converting a data item into the actual address on disk where the item is stored, and then going straight to the data, without having to access any intermediate items. There are various methods of associating locations with data, one of the most effective being the method known as *'hashing'* which applies a calculation to the data to give a disk address. In practice, BASIC's random access files are usually implemented by using an indexed sequential file with an index entry *for every data item*.

Both random and indexed sequential files are significantly more complicated to use in programs than simple serial and sequential files, and therefore will not be used here. If you are interested, you may pursue the theory in books

MORE ADVANCED TOPICS   167

on Data Processing, or the practical aspects in more advanced programming texts.

LOCAL AND GLOBAL VARIABLES AND PARAMETERS

We have frequently met the terms GLOBAL in RM BASIC and SHARED in Turbo Basic, when we have been using programs which involve procedures. Variables which are used in more than one procedure have been listed after the GLOBAL/SHARED command, to show that they are to be treated as the same value, both inside and outside of the current procedure.

As an illustration, consider a program which contains four procedures: A, B, C and D. Procedures A, B, and C are called by the main driving program, while procedure D is called from within procedure B. We may represent this situation in a diagram (see Figure 10.4). This diagram identifies the five separate regions numbered 1-5. Unless they are referred to in a GLOBAL/SHARED statement, each variable is *local* to the region in which it is used. Thus, a variable **Fred** which is assigned to region 1 is not available in regions 2-5. In order to make **Fred** available in region 2, we would need to put the statement **GLOBAL/SHARED Fred** in procedure A (and **GLOBAL Fred** in the main body of the program in RM BASIC). The variable **Fred** will then be available in the region shaded in Figure 10.5. Similarly, in order to made a variable **Jim** available in each of the regions 2 and 4 we would need to use GLOBAL/SHARED in the following places: the main body of the program, procedure A, procedure B, and procedure D. This is because in order to move from one procedure to another, variables must exist *in all intermediate layers*.

We have not really discussed **parameters** in this book, although we have briefly *used* them in Chapter 9. By a parameter we mean a variable or value which must be *passed to* a procedure or function before the procedure or function can be executed. We are all familiar with the square root function in mathematics which finds the value of the number which must be squared to give a particular value. It would be meaningless to give somebody the instruction 'Find the square root' because there is no such thing as *the square root*. Instead we need to say 'Find the square root of 5' or 'Find the square root of 23.8'. Thus the value 5 or 23.8 is given as the value of the **parameter** which the square root function requires.

Other common mathematical functions require parameters; it is meaningless to say 'Find the sine', we must say 'Find the sine of 39 degrees', and so on. When we defined our own functions using DEF FNY(X), we again had a parameter X enclosed in the brackets so that we could subsequently evaluate FNY at *different* values of X. Thus a parameter gives the opportunity to define a function — the value or behaviour of which varies according to the value of the parameter that is passed to it.

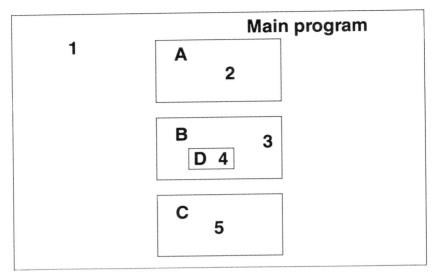

Figure 10.4 The Relationship Between Procedures A, B, C and D Determines Where GLOBAL/SHARED Statements are needed

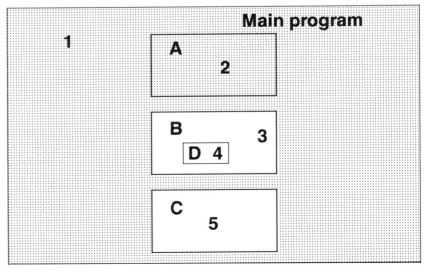

Figure 10.5 The Shaded Area Shows the Availability of a Variable GLOBAL/SHADED Between the Main Program and Procedure A

MORE ADVANCED TOPICS

In a similar way, some versions of BASIC allow the user to write procedures which involve parameters. It might be possible to have a procedure which takes several parameters. Thus we might be able to write a procedure **INVITE** which produces a letter inviting a friend to our house for tea. This procedure could take two parameters: the name of the person we were inviting and the date of the invitation.

The statements for this in Turbo Basic look like this:

SUB Invite(Name$,D$)
PRINT "Dear ";Name$
PRINT "Please come to our house for tea on ";D$
PRINT "Best wishes"
PRINT "Fred"
END SUB

We could then incorporate this in the main program using the statements:

PRINT "Who do you want to invite?"
INPUT Friend$
PRINT "When?"
INPUT Day$
CALL Invite(Friend$,Day$)

Note that the variables used in the main program do not need to have the same names as the names of the parameters listed in the procedure definition. The names can match if you wish, though it is often easier to check for errors if the parameter names used are different. In the example given here, the effect of the CALL instruction is to 'pass' the value of **Friend$** to the parameter **Name$** and the value of the variable **Day$** to the parameter **D$**. The procedure Invite can then refer to **Name$** and **D$** and will recover the values of **Friend$** and **Day$** respectively.

Many programmers recommend the use of parameters in preference to global variables for passing values into procedures and functions, and for those programmers who fully understand how they should be used, this is a very sensible approach. However, many less-sophisticated versions of BASIC do not offer the facility to pass parameters at all, and very few versions of BASIC offer all the facilities required for passing parameters, which would be necessary if global variables were to be eliminated altogether. Using methods of programming which relied too heavily on the passing of parameters would therefore unnecessarily restrict the choice of BASIC language implementation. Once again, the reader with a particular interest in this area should begin by referring to a programmers' reference manual for the particular version in use.

SUMMARY

The facilities described in this chapter are not dealt with in detail here. The interested reader will find more information about the applications of multi-dimensional arrays, random and indexed files and parameter passing in more advanced books on programming in BASIC, or in programmers' reference manuals for the version of the language in use.

11 More Applications

INTRODUCTION

This final chapter has seven realistic and worthwhile exercises which you should now be able to try. The first two exercises are discussed in a little more detail to help you to get started, and the design of a possible solution is given using structure diagrams. In the later exercises the problem is described, but the solution is left entirely to the reader.

HOW TO WORK ON THE EXERCISES

Exactly how you work on this chapter will depend on your personal situation. You may, for example, be using this book as part of a course of study supported by lectures, or as one of several people following a course of directed private study. In either of these situations there are likely to be other people around who will be working on the same problems. Alternatively, you may be using the book on your own. In either situation, it is most important that you should plan your work carefully.

Before you begin to actually write any programs, and certainly before you start to type programs into the computer, you should put your ideas on paper. In each exercise you will need to bear in mind how the data which is needed is to be stored, and the structure of the program which you need to write. Try to follow the good practices which have been illustrated elsewhere in this book, and write your programs in a well-structured way which uses procedures.

If you are fortunate enough to have other people around who are studying programming and following the same programme of study, try to get together to discuss some of the problems described here. You will be surprised how often a problem which you would spend hours solving on your own, can quickly be solved with a friend with whom you can share your insights. Many people learn programming skills much more quickly from other learners than from their teachers!

When you have finished each program, spend some time testing it. Make sure that each of the different routes through the program do work, and ensure that you always get the output that you should no matter what the inputs are. Finally check your screen displays. Try to be critical of your presentation, and try to be constructive — ask yourself 'if I was writing this program again, how could I make it easier to use?'

Below are the exercises:

Exercise A

A dentist wishes to use a computer to send out reminders to his patients for their regular checkups. Write a set of programs which will enable him to do this.

Solution: The dentist will need to maintain a list of patient names together with the details of the months in which the checkups are due. Working on the basis of a six-monthly recall, it will therefore be sufficient to store the names together with a number between 1 and 6. Thus a patient stored as:

John Smith 5

will be recalled for a checkup in months 5 and 11 (May and November).

We shall need to put the data either in data statements or in a disk file and then bring it into two arrays for processing. The disk file would give more flexibility and so this is the choice which we shall adopt. This involves us having three programs:

Program A: to create the initial file.

Program B: to amend the file contents when new patients join and old patients move away.

Program C: to print out the reminders each month.

Figures 11.1a, b and c indicate the design of suitable programs.

Exercise B

Motor insurance quotations are usually based on a points scoring system. A series of questions is asked and each possible answer gives a score according to the risk involved (for example: age of driver, type of car, previous accidents). Write a program which would perform this task.

Solution: We need to begin by designing a series of questions together with appropriate answer and the scores which would be given to each possible answer. (You might like to go and visit an insurance broker to find out what questions would be asked in practice.)

In a situation like this, the user will find it easy to give the required answers if each question is provided with a menu of possible answers. This avoids the possibility that the computer is unable to understand the meaning of a particular

MORE APPLICATIONS 173

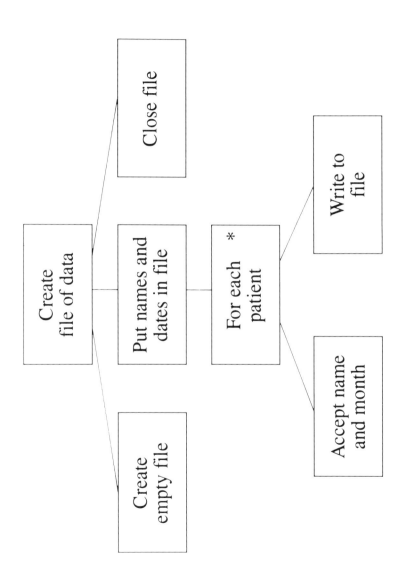

Figure 11.1a   File Create Program

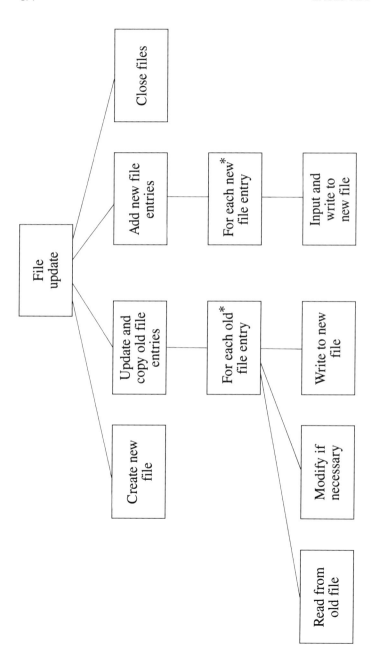

Figure 11.1b The File Update Program Design

MORE APPLICATIONS

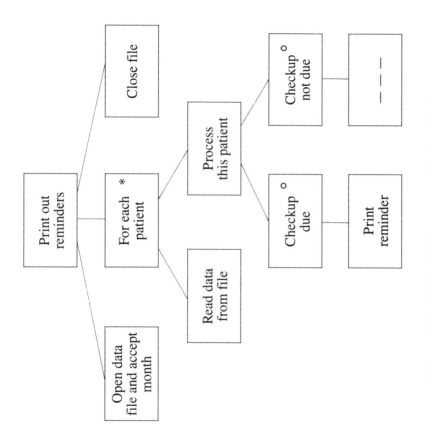

Figure 11.1c Design for Program to Produce Reminders

response because only a selection (eg 1, 2, 3, 4 or 5) corresponding to an acceptable answer can be input.

This program is then quite straightforward (see Figure 11.2). The main points to note are the importance of the initialisation of the score to zero for each client (otherwise the previous client's score will be added on!), and the careful design of the menu procedures so that only valid responses are accepted, and the system is pleasant to use.

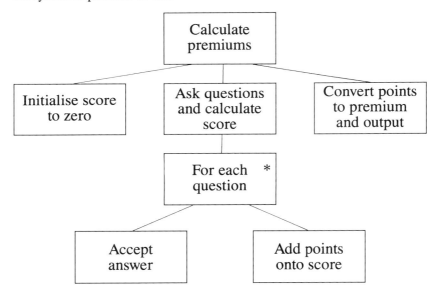

Figure 11.2   Design of Insurance Premium Program

Exercise C

Write a program which operates like a bank ATM (Automated Teller Machine — this is the technical name for a cash dispenser). The program should permit a user to enter an account number and password, and give details of the user's account balance, before allowing a suitable amount to be withdrawn. (NB your bank needs to have several customers!)

Exercise D

Write a program which produces a simulated hand of seven cards and draws them on the screen. You should avoid having the same card appearing more than once in a hand.

Exercise E

A doctor decides to use a computer to store details of regular prescription requests from patients. He wants to maintain a list of patient names, alongside the medicines which they are to receive and the date on which their last prescription was dispensed, so that he can keep a check on double prescriptions. Design and write a suitable package to do this.

Exercise F

You have been employed by an examining board to provide a computer program to produce examination certificates. The program should accept a list of subjects and marks for each named student and print out a certificate giving appropriate grades.

Exercise G

Write a suite of programs which administer a credit card for your friends. You will need to have a question and answer section to assess credit-worthiness and to impose a credit limit for each user, a method of adding items purchased to the current balance owing from a cardholder, a facility to produce regular statements, and the means to adjust the balance when an account is paid.

Appendix 1
Epilogue

After reading this book, you should have a good idea about programming, at least in the BASIC language, and you should also have the confidence to write the sorts of programs that we have discussed here. But we have not been able to cover all the varied aspects of modern BASICs in this book. We have not mentioned the use of sound or animation or the importing of images from elsewhere to produce interesting displays. We have not worked using random access files and so on. It is up to you to decide what sort of programming interests you and then to look into that in more detail.

There are many other books available on BASIC. If you are interested in the practicalities of writing more programs, then I recommend that you get hold of a BASIC reference manual for the particular BASIC that you are using. Some of these are supplied with the language, but often you can get a better one by buying it separately. Some suitable books are listed in Appendix 2. On the other hand, if you are a student of computing, you might be better advised to learn more about programming, systems analysis and design, and software engineering, by reading some of the introductory books listed in this area. Or alternatively, perhaps you feel that you would like to become *bilingual* and learn a second computer language. In this case your choice of book would be governed by your choice of language.

Whatever happens, don't give up now! There's a lot more to learn.

Appendix 2
Bibliography

Books on BASIC

Howard M, *Understanding and Using Microsoft BASIC/IBM PC BASIC*, West Publishing Co, 1987

Research Machines Ltd, *RM BASIC Manual* (editions to support different releases of the language)

Bebbington E, *RM BASIC: An Introduction For Nimbus Users*, NCC Publications, 1989

Wortman L A, *The Power of Turbo Basic*, Tab Books, 1988

Alcock D, *Illustrating BASIC*, CUP, 1986

Borland International, *Turbo Basic Manual*, 1987

Kittner M L, Northcut B, *Basic BASIC: A Structured Approach*, Addison Wesley, 1987

Books on System Analysis and Design, Software Engineering

Oliver E C, Chapman R J, (revised by French C S), *Data Processing* (seventh edition), DP Publications, 1987

Simons G, *Introducing Software Engineering*, NCC Publications, 1987

Davis W S, *Systems Analysis and Design: A Structured Approach*, Addison Wesley, 1983

Sommerville I, *Software Engineering*, Addison Wesley, 1989

Meek B L, Heath P, Rushby N, *Guide to Good Programming Practice* (second edition), Ellis Horwood, 1984

Appendix 3
Answers to Selected Exercises

Program 2.5a RM BASIC version

```
10   REM Program to output screen as in Figure 2.7
20   CLS
30   HOME
40   PRINT "Hello. I'm your friendly computer."
50   PRINT "What's your name?"
60   INPUT Name$
70   PRINT "Do you like computers, ";Name$;"?"
80   INPUT Comp$
90   INPUT "Where do you come from, ";Name$;"?"
100  INPUT Place$
110  PRINT "Do you like ";Place$;" ";Name$;"?"
120  INPUT Like$
130  PRINT "I've got to go now, goodbye."
```

Program 2.5b IBM BASIC version

```
10   REM Program to output screen as in Figure 2.7
20   CLS
30   PRINT "Hello. I'm your friendly computer."
40   PRINT "What's your name?"
50   INPUT Name$
60   PRINT "Do you like computers, ";Name$;"?"
70   INPUT Comp$
80   PRINT "Where do you come from, ";Name$;"?"
90   INPUT Place$
100  PRINT "Do you like ";Place$;" ";Name$;"?"
110  INPUT Like$
120  PRINT "I've got to go now, goodbye."
```

Program 2.7

```
10   REM Program to perform simple VAT calculation
20   CLS
30   HOME {This line needed for RM Basic only}
40   PRINT"            VAT Analysis"
50   PRINT
60   PRINT "This program accepts details of the"
70   PRINT "total amount spent, and the % tax"
80   PRINT "and displays the tax payable."
90   PRINT
100  PRINT "Please type in the amount spent in £"
110  INPUT Amount
120  PRINT "Please type in the VAT rate (%)"
130  INPUT Rate
140  Tax = Amount * Rate / 100
150  PRINT "Total tax payable is £";Tax
```

Program 3.6

```
REM MENU 2
CLS
HOME {Not needed in IBM version}
PRINT
PRINT "Select shape required"
PRINT
PRINT "1.      Square"
PRINT "2.      Triangle"
PRINT "3.      Circle"
PRINT
PRINT
PRINT "Choice:"
INPUT Shape
```

Program 4.6a RM BASIC version

```
10   REM Password 2
20   Count:=0
30   REPEAT
40   CLS
50   HOME
60   PRINT "Type in your password"
70   INPUT Pass$
80   Count:=Count+1
90   UNTIL(Pass$="Chester")
100  PRINT "Password accepted, welcome to the program."
```

ANSWERS TO SELECTED EXERCISES

Program 4.6b Turbo Basic version

```
10   REM Password 2
20   Count=0
30   DO
40   CLS
50   PRINT "Type in your password"
60   INPUT Pass$
70   Count=Count+1
80   LOOP UNTIL(Pass$="Chester") OR (Pass$="CHESTER")
     OR (Pass$="chester") OR (Count=3)
90   PRINT "Password accepted, welcome to the program."
```

Program 4.6c IBM BASICA version

```
10   REM Password
20   Count=0
30   Pass$="rubbish"
40   WHILE(Pass$<>"Chester") AND (Pass$<> "CHESTER")
     AND (Pass$ <> "chester") AND (Count <> 3)
50   CLS
60   PRINT "Type in your password"
70   INPUT Pass$
80   Count=Count+1
90   WEND
100  PRINT "Password accepted, welcome to the program."
```

Program 4.7a RM BASIC version

```
10   REM Shop program
20   CLS
30   HOME
40   Count =-1
50   Ttal=0
60   REPEAT
70   PRINT "Type in next sum of money, 0 to finish"
80   INPUT Amount
90   Ttal=Ttal+Amount
100  Count=Count+1
110  UNTIL Amount=0
120  PRINT "Total sales : ";Ttal
130  PRINT "Total assistants : ";Count
140  PRINT "Average takings : ";Ttal/Count
```

Program 4.7b Turbo Basic version

```
10   REM Shop program
20   CLS
30   Count=-1
40   Ttal=0
50   DO
60   PRINT "Type in next sum of money, 0 to finish"
70   INPUT Amount
80   Ttal=Ttal+Amount
90   Count=Count+1
100  LOOP UNTIL Amount=0
110  PRINT "Total sales : ";Ttal
120  PRINT "Total assistants : ";Count
130  PRINT "Average takings : ";Ttal/Count
```

Program 4.7c IBM BASICA version

```
10   REM Shop program
20   CLS
30   Count =-1
40   Ttal=0
50   Amount =-1
60   WHILE Amount<>0
70   PRINT "Type in next sum of money, 0 to finish"
80   INPUT Amount
90   Ttal=Ttal+Amount
100  Count=Count+1
110  WEND
120  PRINT "Total sales : ";Ttal
130  PRINT "Total assistants :";Count
140  PRINT "Average takings : ";Ttal/Count
```

Note: the initial value of Count = −1 in Programs 4.7a, b and c results in the final value being correct. (Try it and see!)

Program 5.6a RM BASIC version

```
10   REM Party Invitation Program
20   GLOBAL Name$,Place$,T$,D$,Guest$
30   Partyinfo
40   Guestinfo
50   Invite
60   END
70   PROCEDURE Partyinfo
80   GLOBAL Name$,Place$,T$,D$
90   PRINT "Type in the name of the person whose party it is"
```

```
100 INPUT Name$
110 PRINT "Type in the place where party is to be held"
120 INPUT Place$
130 PRINT "Type in the date of the party"
140 INPUT D$
150 PRINT "Type in starting time for the party"
160 INPUT T$
170 ENDPROC
180 PROCEDURE Guestinfo
190   GLOBAL Guest$
200   PRINT "Type in guest's name"
210   INPUT "Guest$
220 ENDPROC
230 PROCEDURE Invite
240   GLOBAL Name$,Place$,T$,D$,Guest$
250   CLS
260   HOME
270   PRINT "Come to a party";Guest$
280   PRINT "on ";D$,T$
290   PRINT "at ";Place$
300   PRINT "Please come!"
310   PRINT "from ";Name$
320 ENDPROC
```

Program 5.6b Turbo Basic version

```
REM Party Invitation Program
CALL Partyinfo
CALL Guestinfo
CALL Invite
END
SUB Partyinfo
  SHARED Name$,Place$,T$,D$
  PRINT "Type in the name of the person whose party it is"
  INPUT Name$
  PRINT "Type in the place where party is to be held"
  INPUT Place$
  PRINT "Type in the date of the party"
  INPUT D$
  PRINT "Type in starting time for party"
  INPUT T$
END SUB
SUB Guestinfo
  SHARED Guest$
```

```
PRINT "Type in guest's name"
INPUT Guest$
END SUB
SUB Invite
SHARED Name$,Place$,T$,D$,Guest$
CLS
PRINT "Come to a party ";Guest$
PRINT "on ";D$,T$
PRINT "at ";Place$
PRINT "Please come!"
PRINT "from ";Name$
END SUB
```

Program 5.6c IBM BASICA version

```
10   REM Party Invitation
20   GOSUB 1000 : REM Partyinfo
30   GOSUB 2000 : REM Guestinfo
40   GOSUB 3000 : REM Invite
50   END
1000 REM Partyinfo
1010 PRINT "Type in the name of the person whose party it is"
1020 INPUT Name$
1030 PRINT "Type in the place where party is to be held"
1040 INPUT Place$
1050 PRINT "Type in the date of the party"
1060 INPUT D$
1070 PRINT "Type in starting time for the party"
1080 INPUT T$
1999 RETURN
2000 REM Guestinfo
2010 PRINT "Type in guest's name"
2020 INPUT Guest$
2030 RETURN
3000 REM Invite
3010 CLS
3020 PRINT "Come to a party ";Guest$
3030 PRINT "on ";D$,T$
3040 PRINT "at ";Place$
3050 PRINT "Please come!"
3060 PRINT "from ";Name$
3070 RETURN
```

Program 5.10a RM BASIC version

```
10   REM Party Invitation Program
20   GLOBAL Name$,Place$,T$,D$,Guest$( ),Guestno
30   Partyinfo
40   Guestinfo
50   Invite
60   END
70   PROCEDURE Partyinfo
80   GLOBAL Name$,Place$,T$,D$
90   PRINT "Type in the name of the person whose party it is"
100  INPUT Name$
110  PRINT "Type in the place where party is to be held"
120  INPUT Place$
130  PRINT "Type in the date of the party"
140  INPUT D$
150  PRINT "Type in starting time for the party"
160  INPUT T$
170  ENDPROC
180  PROCEDURE Guestinfo
190  GLOBAL Guest$( ), Guestno
200  PRINT "How many guests are there to be?"
210  INPUT Guestno
220  DIM Guest$(Guestno)
230  FOR I=1 to Guestno
240  PRINT "Type in guest number ";I
250  INPUT Guest$(I)
260  NEXT I
270  ENDPROC
280  PROCEDURE Invite
290  GLOBAL Name$,Place$,T$,D$,Guest$( ),Guestno
300  FOR I=1 TO Guestno
310  CLS
320  HOME
330  PRINT "Come to a party ";Guest$(I)
340  PRINT "on ";D$,T$
350  PRINT "at ";Place$
360  PRINT "Please come!"
370  PRINT "from ";Name$
380  NEXT I
390  ENDPROC
```

Program 5.10b Turbo Basic version

```
REM Party Invitation Program
CALL PARTYINFO
CALL GUESTINFO
CALL INVITE
END
SUB Partyinfo
SHARED Name$,Place$,T$,D$
PRINT "Type in the name of the person whose party it is"
INPUT Name$
PRINT "Type in the place where party is to be held"
INPUT Place$
PRINT "Type in the date of the party"
INPUT D$
PRINT "Type in starting time for the party"
INPUT T$
END SUB
SUB Guestinfo
SHARED Guest$( ),Guestno
PRINT "How many guests are there to be?"
INPUT Guestno
DIM Guest$(Guestno)
FOR I=1 TO Guestno
PRINT "Type in guest number ";I
INPUT Guest$(I)
NEXT I
END SUB
SUB Invite
SHARED Name$,Place$,T$,D$,Guest$( ),Guestno
FOR I=1 TO Guestno
CLS
PRINT "Come to a party ";Guest$(I)
PRINT "on ";D$,T$
PRINT "at ";Place$
PRINT "Please come!"
PRINT "from ";Name$
NEXT I
END SUB
```

Program 5.10c IBM BASICA version

```
10  REM Party Invitation
20  GOSUB 1000 : REM Partyinfo
30  GOSUB 2000 : REM Guestinfo
```

```
  40   GOSUB 3000 : REM Invite
  50   END
1000   REM Partyinfo
1010   PRINT "Type in the name of the name of the person whose
       party it is"
1020   INPUT Name$
1030   PRINT "Type in the place where party is to be held"
1040   INPUT Place$
1050   PRINT "Type in the date of the party"
1060   INPUT D$
1070   PRINT "Type in starting time for the party"
1080   INPUT T$
1999   RETURN
2000   REM Guestinfo
2010   PRINT "How many guests are there to be?"
2020   INPUT Guestno
2030   DIM Guest$(Guestno)
2040   FOR I=1 TO Guestno
2050   PRINT "Type in guest number ";I
2060   INPUT Guest$(I)
2070   NEXT I
2080   RETURN
3000   REM Invite
3010   FOR I = 1 TO Guestno
3020   CLS
3030   PRINT "Come to a party ";Guest$(I)
3040   PRINT "on ";D$,T$
3050   PRINT "at ";Place$
3060   PRINT "Please come!"
3070   PRINT "from ";Name$
3080   NEXT I
3090   RETURN
```

Program 5.11a RM BASIC version

```
10   REM Letters Program
20   GLOBAL Personname$( ),Number
30   Personlist
40   Letter
50   END
60   PROCEDURE Personlist
70   GLOBAL Personname$( ), Number
80   PRINT "How many letters do you require?"
90   INPUT Number
```

```
100  DIM Personname$(Number)
110  FOR I=1 TO Number
120  PRINT "Type in name number ";I
130  INPUT Personname$(I)
140  NEXT I
150  ENDPROC
160  PROCEDURE Letter
170  GLOBAL Personname$( ),Number
180  FOR I=1 TO Number
190  PRINT "Dear "; Personname(I)
200  PRINT "Please come to tea on Saturday"
210  PRINT "        Yours"
220  NEXT I
230  ENDPROC
```

Program 5.11b Turbo Basic version

```
10   REM Letters program
20   CALL Personlist
30   CALL Letter
40   END
50   SUB Personlist
60   SHARED Personname$( ),Number
70   PRINT "How many letters do you require?"
80   INPUT Number
90   DIM Personname$(Number)
100  FOR I=1 TO Number
110  PRINT "Type in name number ";I
120  INPUT Personname$(I)
130  NEXT I
140  END SUB
150  SUB Letter
160  SHARED Personname$( ),Number
170  FOR I=1 TO Number
180  PRINT "Dear ";Personname(I)
190  PRINT "Please come to tea on Saturday"
200  PRINT "        Yours"
210  NEXT I
220  END SUB
```

Program 5.11c IBM BASIC version

```
10   REM Letters program
20   GOSUB 1000 : REM Personlist
30   GOSUB 2000 : REM Letter
40   END
```

ANSWERS TO SELECTED EXERCISES 193

```
1000  REM Personlist
1010  PRINT "How many letters do you require?"
1020  INPUT Number
1030  DIM Personname$(Number)
1040  FOR I=1 TO Number
1050  PRINT "Type in name number ";I
1060  INPUT Personname$(I)
1070  NEXT I
1080  RETURN
2000  REM Letter
2010  FOR I=1 TO Number
2020  PRINT "Dear ";Personname(I)
2030  PRINT "Please come to tea on Saturday"
2040  PRINT "          Yours"
2050  NEXT I
2060  RETURN
```

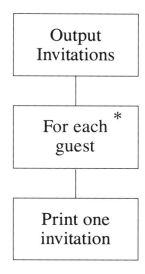

Figure 6.7 Structure Diagram for Procedure Invite

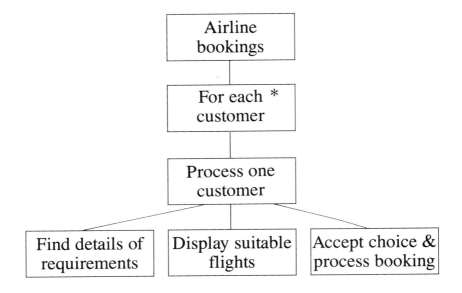

Figure 6.14 Structure Diagram for Simple Airline Booking System

Program 8.1

The following are the RM BASIC procedures needed to adapt the program listed at 7.19 to the specification of Figure 8.6. The modifications to the Turbo and IBM programs are similar.

```
PROCEDURE Processcustomers
GLOBAL Thisorder,Itemno,Cat$,Catno$( ),Desc$( ),Price( ),Order$( ),
Index( ),Totsales,Counter
REPEAT
REM (Input list of items required)
Thisorder=0
Itemno=1
REPEAT
Dataentry
Order$(Itemno)=Cat$
Information
Index(Itemno)=Counter
Givequantity
Numberreq(Itemno)=Quantity
```

```
Itemno=Itemno+1
UNTIL (Itemno=5) OR (Cat$="000/0000")
REM (Process the order)
Itemno=1
REPEAT
Receipt1
Update1
Itemno=Itemno+1
UNTIL (Itemno=5) OR (Cat$="000/0000")
PRINT # 2 Thisorder
UNTIL Order$(1) = "999/9999"
```

The procedures *Information*, *Givequantity* and *Dataentry* are as listed in Program 7.10

```
PROCEDURE Receipt
GLOBAL Numberreq( ),Itemno,Desc$( ),Price( ),Index( )
PRINT # 2 Numberreq(Itemno),Desc$(Index(Itemno));" at
";Price(Index(Itemno));"=";Numberreq(Itemno)*Price(Index
(Itemno))
ENDPROC
PROCEDURE Update
GLOBAL Numberreq( ),Itemno,Index( ),Price( ),Totsales,Thisorder
Sale=Numberreq(Itemno)*Price(Index(Itemno))
Totsales=Totsales+Sale
Thisorder=Thisorder+Sale
ENDPROC
```

Index

accuracy (vs. speed)	161
Ada	5
ALGOL68	5
algorithm	139
analyst/programmer	97
AND	59
AREA	30, 155
arrays	72-73, 101-102, 131, 163
assignment statements	61
body (of loop)	56-57
bugs	17
CALL	45, 48
case sensitivity	59
character	19
checking	60-61
CIRCLE (RM)	30
CIRCLE (IBM)	36
CLOSE	136-138
CLS	15, 18
COBOL	5, 166
code	17
compilation	11
compiler	2, 12
concatenation	42
control variable	75
CREATE	136

DATA	103
data	21
data file	135
data processing	4, 139, 167
data structure	131
DEF FN	160
design of programs	90-95
dialect	4, 8
DIM	73, 133, 163
directory	13
disk	13, 135
disk drive	9
DO . . . LOOP UNTIL	56
driving routine/program	67, 71
dummy entry	138
DUMP	66
editor	11
line	11
screen	11
ENDPROC	53
END SUB	53
errors	
typing	16-17
logical	17
error message	16
execution	11
exit condition	56
expression	158
file	13, 14, 135-146
indexed	166
random access	135, 166
serial	135
sequential	135
updating	142
flowcharts	83-84
formatting	22
FOR . . . NEXT	65, 73-81
FORTRAN	2, 4
functions	
defining	160
mathematical	147

INDEX

GLOBAL	53, 69, 76
GOSUB	53
graphics	27-53, 150-160
modes	27
screen layout	27
hardware configuration	9
hashing	166
HOME	15, 18
identifier	19
IF	45
incrementation	60, 61
information	21
initialisation	18, 58, 60, 61, 99, 114
INPUT	15, 19, 21, 39
INT	149
interactive	18, 19, 23
interpretation	11
interpreter	2, 11, 12
iteration	88, 89, 91
Jackson's structure diagrams	83, 85-96
key records	166
keyboard	9
language	1, 8
high-level	1, 2
low-level	2
general-purpose	6
LINE	35, 150
line number	16
LIST	15-16
lists	71-72
local variables	167
LOCATE	36, 152
LOOP UNTIL	56
loop	55
condition controlled	55-63, 106, 138
count controlled	55, 65, 75, 138
looping	55-63
LPRINT	66

memory	11, 16, 19
menu	43
menu-driven	43
microcomputer	2
Modula-2	5
monitor	9
NEW	15, 16
number	19, 24
object code	11, 12
OPEN	136-8
OR	59
outline program	133
output	17, 18, 27, 39
PAINT	35, 155
parameters	167, 169
Pascal	5
pixel	38
PLOT	32, 152
PRINT	15, 16, 18, 19, 21, 22, 38, 136-137
printer	9, 18, 65-67, 76
PROCEDURE	53
procedure	43, 53, 68, 71, 130
processor	9
program	6, 11, 42, 43
program file	135
Prolog	5
pseudo-random numbers	148-149
random access file	135, 166
random numbers	149
READ	103
refinement	90
REM	15, 17
RENAME	141, 143, 144
REPEAT	56
repeat	56
repetition:	
representation in structure diagram	88
residual value	114
resolution	27

INDEX

RETURN	53
rogue value	111
RND	149
RUN	15, 16
saving files	14
SCREEN	35
screen	15, 18, 27
dump	65, 66
layout	27-53
security	55
selection	43, 88, 89
sequence	88, 89
SET BORDER	30
SET BRUSH	30
SET CURPOS	32
SET MODE	30
SET PAPER	30
SET PEN	30
SET PLOT SIZE	32
SHARED	53, 69, 76
simulation	147
software	42
software engineering	179
source code	11, 12
STEP	161
stepwise refinement	90
string	19, 101
structure diagram	47, 83, 85-96, 133
SUB	53
subprogram	53
subroutine	53
syntax	11
systems analyst	97
table	163
text co-ordinates	34, 36
top-down design	90
translation	2, 9, 12
UNTIL	56
update (file)	142
variable	22, 23

well-structured	43, 83, 130
WEND	57, 145
WHILE	57, 145